Pages of the Past

Exploring U.S. History
Through Children's Literature

Diane Findlay

UpstartBooks

Fort Atkinson, Wisconsin

Where would we be without public libraries? There are several that I use regularly, and I don't know what I'd do without them. Special thanks to the West Des Moines and Waukee Public Libraries, whose collections and wonderful staff members supported me through every step of this process. I'm also grateful to several teacher friends who have served as resources and sounding boards through this and other projects. You know who you are! Thank you.

Credits:

The following organizations have generously given permission to reprint activities in this book:

Pages 11–13: Quoits and Native American Stick Toss from *Colonial Days: Discover the Past with Fun Projects, Games, Activities and Recipes*, © 1997 by David C. King. Reprinted with permission of John Wiley & Sons, Inc.

Pages 33–34: Tin Punch Craft from *A Pioneer Sampler* by Barbara Greenwood. Illustrations © 1994 by Heather Collins/Glyphics. Reprinted with permission of Houghton Mifflin Company. All rights reserved.

Pages 43–44: Wigwag Message from *The Civil War for Kids: A History with 21 Activities*, © 1999 by Janis Herbert. Reprinted with permission of Chicago Review Press.

Pages 56–58: Pebble Target Game and Sand-Dried Flowers from *Victorian Days: Discover the Past with Fun Projects, Games, Activities and Recipes*, © 2000 by David C. King. Reprinted with permission of John Wiley & Sons, Inc.

Published by UpstartBooks
W5527 Highway 106
P.O. Box 800
Fort Atkinson, Wisconsin 53538-0800
1-800-448-4887

© Diane Findlay, 2002
Cover design: Debra Neu Sletten

The paper used in this publication meets the minimum requirements of American National Standard for Information Science — Permanence of Paper for Printed Library Material. ANSI/NISO Z39.48-1992.

Contents

Introduction

The study of history is a complicated proposition. Even the best elementary and middle school textbooks are confined by limits of the genre. They must present a great deal of verifiable information, which conforms to standards of acceptability and community values, in a comprehensive and concise way. Yet every story worth remembering as history was experienced and passed on by people with varied points of view and different emotional responses to the events.

Dr. Lynda G. Adamson, chair of the English Department at Prince George's Community College in Largo, Maryland, has authored several reference bibliographies of literature titles to enrich the study of history. In the introduction to her *Literature Connections to American History: Resources to Enhance and Entice* series, Adamson says,

> Studies show that people must respond emotionally to something in order to remember it. If young readers travel with Fawn in Whelan's *Night of the Full Moon* as U.S. federal troops remove … her Potawatomi tribe from their ancestral home, or if they look at the torn and dirty books 'discarded' from the white school that Cassie's teacher must issue to Cassie and her classmates in Taylor's *Roll of Thunder, Hear My Cry,* they will wonder why some laws can favor one group over another. By becoming angry … these readers remember the time and place of the incidents… These vicarious experiences could even help readers empathize more readily with the difficulties of contemporary refugees or the hostility of people whose families have lived in America for many decades.

The dreams, ambitions, disappointments, tragedies and joys of fictional characters, or of historical figures shared in biography, bring history alive and imbue the facts with human significance and relevance. Through exposure to compelling characters (especially young ones) in well-chosen fiction, biography or trade nonfiction, students begin to imagine what it might have been like to share in the experiences that shaped—and continue to shape—our nation. And as Dr. Adamson implies, where a student's emotions and imagination are engaged, empathy can grow and be transferred and applied to events and issues in contemporary life.

We study history to learn who we are and where we have been. We study history to appreciate the sacrifices and achievements of those who came before us, to learn from their mistakes and to nurture healthy, involved citizens who have an informed sense of what we need to do differently and better as we mature as a nation. It is the human element—the ability to understand cause and effect at a human level—which motivates us, as individuals and as a society, to move toward fulfilling those goals.

Literature helps us engage students at a personal level by taking the abstract concepts in our history texts and showing how they impacted people's lives. Imagine the lively and meaningful discussion that could result from reading about the Salem witch trials from the perspectives of specific child accusers, the accused and the judges! Not only does such discussion actively engage students, but it also stimulates critical thinking skills such as compare and contrast, analysis, evaluation and synthesis.

This book is designed to help educators find and use good literature to engage students and enrich the study of U.S. history. The target audience is teachers of grades four through eight, during which time U.S. history is most often presented in the curriculum. The eight chapters cover key events and periods in American history that share not only proximity in time, but also common themes and issues. The titles included in each annotated bibliography reflect the themes and issues of that chapter and period. They were chosen for their potential to engage the imagination, elicit emotional responses, challenge students to think from a new perspective, stimulate an interest in further reading and learning or create opportunities for students to relate events from the past to issues in the present. For each period, I have tried to include compelling and appealing characters, glimpses of everyday life and explorations of social issues of the times. The suggested activities are designed to further involve students in the ideas and activities that characterized the period and to give them opportunities to express and exchange their new thoughts and insights. My hope is that through use of these books and activities, every student will find something that "clicks"—that makes a connection between stories of the seemingly distant past and his or her life and interests.

The books listed are the best examples I could find in the riches of contemporary and classic children's literature that serve the intended purpose. You'll see award winners, classics, hot-off-the-press titles, fiction and nonfiction and a variety of media and reading levels. Some high-quality picture books are included as well. They can be read aloud to introduce or summarize periods or concepts, or used to stimulate interest in visual learners or reluctant readers. They may not be age appropriate in all classrooms, but they might be just right for your class or someone in it. All titles are in print or readily available in libraries. I encourage you to add your own favorites to the lists and to adapt the activity ideas to suit you, your students and your situation. Both the books and the activities are offered for use in a variety of groupings and settings.

Finally, I'd like to recommend a few specific resources that could be useful supplements to your exploration of U.S. history. In *Hand in Hand: An American History through Poetry* (collected by Lee Bennett Hopkins, Simon & Schuster, 1994), the choice of poems and poets from different periods of our nation's history combined with the lovely illustrations in lush picture book format make for an appealing resource. In *We Were There, Too! Young People in U.S. History* (by Phillip Hoose, Farrar, Straus and Giroux, 2001) the roles of nearly 70 specific young people from our national history are traced through photos, quotations and biographical narrative. Chronological chapters place the individuals in time and the writing is concise and accessible. *From Sea to Shining Sea: A Treasury of American Folklore and Folk Songs* (compiled by Amy L. Cohn, Scholastic, 1993) is exactly what it claims to be—a rich collection of stories, poems, songs and delightful illustrations that highlight the nation's folk history from creation through the 1960s. Finally, the History in Song Web site (www.fortunecity.com/tinpan/parton/2/history.html) offers songs to listen to as well as information about particular compositions and performers, from the American Revolution through the 1960s.

A note about Web sites: Because Web sites are constantly evolving, teachers and students are advised to perform a keyword search on the Web site title if the URL provided does not bring the site up.

Colonial America

The colonial period in America, approximately 1600–1775, was a time of contradictions and conflicting interests, hardships, hard work and homemade pleasures. It was largely spurred by conditions in Europe and played out against the background of shifting loyalties and conflicts in "the old country." It called forth both the highest and lowest in human motives and behaviors, as lofty idealism and opportunistic greed, friendliness and fear worked their results in the lives of the colonists, explorers, missionaries, traders, Native Americans, indentured servants and African slaves.

Some themes of this period to explore through literature include:

★ The colonists: Where did they come from and why?

★ How did colonists interact with each other?

★ Who was already living on the land, and how did the colonists interact with them?

★ Religious freedom for whom?

★ Changing relationships with the mother country.

★ Everyday life in the colonies.

★ Supplying labor: Indentured servitude and slavery.

Many publishers of children's books offer series that deal with aspects of life during and after colonial times. In some cases, where series titles seemed the best choices to serve the purpose and round out the chapter, I have included individual books from a series in the bibliography. You might look for additional titles, in response to specific needs or interests, from appropriate series. The following is just a sampling; your school media center or public libraries may have others.

★ American Kids in History by David C. King. John Wiley & Sons, Inc. 3–7.

★ Colonial Craftsmen by Leonard Everett Fisher. Marshall Cavendish, Inc. 4–6.

★ Colonial Leaders. Chelsea House Publishers. 4–7.

★ Dear America. Scholastic. 5–8.

★ Historic Communities by Bobbie Kalman. Crabtree Publishing. 4–7.

★ History Mysteries. Pleasant Company Publications. 5–8.

Resources on Colonial America

★Fiction

★ *Feathertop: Based on the Tale by Nathaniel Hawthorne* by Robert D. San Souci. Bantam Doubleday Dell Books for Young Readers, 1995. 4–6. Mother Rigby, a powerful witch, creates a magical scarecrow too fine to set in the field. She sends "Feathertop" to court the daughter of one of her tormentors as a retaliatory joke. But when Feathertop and the young lady fall in love, Mother Rigby must consider whether any magic can make him truly human. This retelling of Nathaniel Hawthorne's story by the award-winning San Souci brothers sheds light on colonial life and timeless human emotions.

★ *Hester Bidgood, Investigatrix of Evill Deedes* by E. W. Hildick. Macmillan, 1994. 4–8. When Goody Willson's cat is found tortured and she is accused as a witch, young Hester and her friend Rob go sleuthing to discover the real culprit. Considering that the penalty for convicted witches is often death, Hester's determination and Rob's Indian-trained tracking skills are needed to save the day.

★ *The Matchlock Gun* by Walter D. Edmonds. Putnam, 1998. 4–6. Newbery Medal Book. This 1941 title is old enough that some language may seem insensitive, but it tells a gripping story of the courage of a young Dutch settler boy and his mother who must protect their family from an Indian raid during the French and Indian Wars. A quick and easy read for younger students.

★ *My Brother, My Enemy* by Madge Harrah. Simon & Schuster Books for Young Readers, 1997. 5–8. Harrah describes the 1676 Bacon Rebellion from the viewpoint of a 14-year-old Virginia boy. Robert is torn between Bacon's compelling passion for independence from England and revenge against the Indians, who murdered Robert's family; and his Susquehannock blood brother and sister, who tried to save his family. A dramatic story, full of action and detail about events of the period.

★ *Roanoke: A Novel of the Lost Colony* by Sonia Levitin. Simon & Schuster, 2000. 6–8. Twenty years before the establishment of the first permanent British colony in America, a group left England to settle at Chesapeake. They ended up on Roanoke instead and eventually disappeared with hardly a trace in a mystery that is unsolved to this day. This engaging novel tells what might have happened through the eyes of William Wythers, a believable, appealing young rebel whose adventures and trials bring the wilderness of pre-colonized America to life.

★ *Saturnalia* by Paul Fleischman. Harper Trophy, 2001. 6–8. Fleischman takes us to Boston in 1681, through a series of interweaving plots involving memorable characters. The main character is William, a Narraganset Indian of 14, captured six years earlier and apprenticed to a kind and freethinking printer. The life suits William. Still, part of him longs for his lost family and way of life. Shifting the scene between day and night and the tone from humorous to eerie, Fleischman deftly creates a mosaic of action and images likely to engage more sophisticated readers.

★ *The Secret of the Sachem's Tree* by F. N. Monjo. Coward, McGann & Geoghegan, 1972. 4–5. Although an advanced easy reader, this title tells a complicated story in an interesting way. The author elaborates on a tale, cherished in Connecticut, about hiding the Connecticut Colonial Charter issued by King Charles II in order to foil a plot by his successor, King James II, to rescind the privileges of the charter. A delightful and fascinating taste of the flavor of colonial life.

★ *The 13th Floor: A Ghost Story* by Sid Fleischman. Bantam Doubleday Dell, 1997. 4–7. Twelve-year-old Buddy and his older sister are drawn back three centuries in time to rescue their ancestors from the gallows— one as an accused witch and the other as a marauding pirate! Likable, spunky characters carry this cheerful story which provides considerable detail about colonial times while taking the reader on a romp through life, liberty and the pursuit of buried treasure.

★ *The Witch of Blackbird Pond* by Elizabeth George Speare. Houghton Mifflin, 2001. 6–8. Newbery Medal Book. Kit grew up in Barbados, but after the death of her family, she fled to Connecticut to escape an arranged marriage. Our free-spirited heroine has trouble fitting into life with her strict Puritan relatives, and stirs disapproval and suspicion when she befriends a Quaker woman suspected of witchcraft. Speare stirringly evokes the complex political and religious issues of the time, in the context of strong characters, compelling relationships, dramatic conflict and romance.

★ Nonfiction

★ *Amos Fortune, Free Man* by Elizabeth Yates. Troll, 1999. 4–8. Newbery Medal Book. With a 1950 copyright, this title does not reflect twenty-first-century political correctness, but it deserves its place. It is the true story of a young African chieftain, kidnapped and sold into slavery in America, who manages to buy his freedom (and that of several other slaves) and become a model of gentleness, patience and dignity for people of any age, gender or race. His story is not filled with violence, abuse, hatred or anger, and thus adds the balance of a moderating voice to discussion of the period.

★ *Colonial Cooking* by Susan Dosier. Blue Earth Books, 2000. 4–6. Foods and recipes are the focus for glimpses into life in the colonies, as well as social commentary on such issues as the contribution of Native Americans to colonial life and the treatment of African slaves. Interesting narrative, a good list of Web sites and clear cooking directions make this useful. An Exploring History through Simple Recipes series title.

★ *Colonial Days: Discover the Past with Fun Projects, Games, Activities and Recipes* by David C. King. John Wiley & Sons, Inc., 1998. 4–7. Life in colonial Massachusetts is seen through the eyes of the fictional Mayhew family. Each chapter reflects a season, describing daily events and offering interesting projects with easy-to-follow instructions. Activities should interest a wide range of ages, but constant reference to "having an adult help…" may limit the appeal to older students.

★ *The Double Life of Pocahontas* by Jean Fritz. Penguin Putnam, 2002. 4–8. This biography debunks romantic notions of the Disney version, explaining that Pocahontas may have saved John Smith's life as part of a traditional adoption ceremony. Fritz describes Pocahontas's life caught between two cultural worlds, both of which used her for their own purposes.

★ *The First Thanksgiving* by Jean Craighead George. Putnam, 1996. 4–8. Award-winning artist Thomas Locker commissioned this story from Newbery-winner George so he could illustrate it! The result is a beautiful Children's Book-of-the-Month-Club picture book featuring Locker's fine paintings and George's rich, sensitive and historically credible text. This version offers unusual insight into the geology of Plymouth Rock and the background of Native American life in the area, along with the history and role of Squanto.

★ *The New Americans: Colonial Times, 1620–1689* by Betsy and Giulio Maestro. HarperCollins Children's Books, 1998. 4–8. The Maestros produce another excellent overview of a topic in American history as part of their American Story series. This book focuses on Native Americans already here when the Pilgrims landed and the interactions among the Indians; British colonists; and French, Spanish, Dutch and Swedish settlers. Effective paintings and maps enhance understanding and animate the story.

★ *Outrageous Women of Colonial America* by Mary Rodd Furbee. John Wiley & Sons, Inc., 2001. 4–8. This lighthearted, visually appealing book gives brief accounts of the lives of 14 remarkable colonial and Revolutionary era women. Anne Hutchinson, Abigail Adams, Phillis Wheatley and Betsy Ross appear, along with less well-known characters. The style is informal, humorous and a bit "slangy." The extraordinary stories may inspire students to dig deeper into the lives of these gutsy, unconventional women.

★ *The Pilgrims of Plimoth* by Marcia Sewall. Simon & Schuster, 1996. 4–8. Sewall's tale of the journey from England to Plimoth and the first 10 years of the colony is told in lovely illustrations and language that evokes the time and place. A glossary defines unfamiliar words in the text. Chapters could be presented in costumed dramatic reading format. Sewall has won numerous awards for her picture books on the history of New England.

★ *A Sampler View of Colonial Life with Projects Kids Can Make* by Mary Cobb. Millbrook Press, 2000. 4–6. Cobb shares much about the education of girls in colonial times through exploring the use of sewn and hand-printed samplers at home and in dame, district and seminary schools. Good illustrations and projects with patterns and simple directions make this book fun.

★ ***Stranded at Plimoth Plantation 1626*** by Gary Bowen. HarperCollins, 1998. 4–8. Christopher Sears, a 13-year-old orphan, is stranded at Plimoth after the ship that was to deliver him as an indentured servant to Jamestown is destroyed. Journal entries cover most of a year, relating Sears's experience of the seasons, birth, death, weddings, drilling with the militia, illness, farming and other hardships and joys of life in the New World. The journal format, which may catch the interest of students, is richly supported by Bowen's beautiful woodcuts, which are attributed to Sears in the story. A beautiful "advanced picture book" experience, as well as an interesting, informative read.

★ ***Tituba*** by William Miller. Harcourt, 2000. 4–8. This account of the life of West Indian slave Tituba, who was among those convicted as witches in Salem, Massachusetts, is fictionalized from scant details known about her life. It adds depth to our understanding of where the early Americans came from and why. Vibrant illustrations stimulate the imagination.

★ ***William Penn: Founder of Pennsylvania*** by Steven Kroll. Holiday House, 2000. 4–6. This picture book biography of William Penn, Quaker and founder of Pennsylvania, stresses Penn's willingness to give up his life of privilege to stand up for his beliefs. By turns favored and persecuted in England, Penn spent much of his life imprisoned for his convictions. Still, his influence on the government of Pennsylvania was enduring, and his ownership of the colony lasted until the Revolution. A good look at issues in England that caused people to seek religious freedom in the colonies.

Other Media

★ ***Colonial & Revolution Songs*** by Keith and Rusty McNeil. WEM Records, 1989 (two audiocassettes). 4–8. Folk songs from colonial and revolutionary days are introduced with brief, informative commentary. Simple arrangements add to their authenticity and appeal. Use this as background, for sing-along breaks or for study.

★ ***Jamestown.*** From the Colonial Life for Children series produced by Schlessinger Media, 1998 (videocassette, 23 minutes). 4–7. This slick, visually appealing video features Greg, a young student researching a school assignment, who is transported through his computer to the Jamestown Museum. Costumed interpreters guide him through the ships that brought the original Jamestown settlers, the settlement itself and a nearby Powhatan village. A clever concept and a fast-paced, "high tech" introduction to the tragedies and achievements of the first permanent English colony in the New World.

★ ***The Light in the Forest***, by Conrad Richter, narrated by Robert Sean Leonard. Bantam Audio, 1992 (two audiocassettes). 5–8. This is an excellent recording of the powerful classic about a young white boy abducted and raised by Lenape Indians, who is returned to his white family against his will. He resents and resists his white family's claims on him and their attitude toward Indian "savages." Yet when he returns to his tribe he learns that they, too, have elements of treachery and violence among them. The hatred and misunderstandings between natives and whites in colonial times are made clear and comprehensible; the good and evil in both camps is fairly portrayed. A troubling, thought-provoking story.

Web sites

★ ***Colonial Albany Image Gallery*** www.nysm.nysed.gov/albany/gallery.html

★ ***Colonial Era Photos*** www.mohicanpress.com/mo08020.html

★ ***A Colonial Family and Community*** www.hfmgv.org/education/smartfun/ colonial/intro

★ ***Colonial Williamsburg*** www.history.org/ *(click on "history," then "electronic fieldtrips")*

★ ***Long Island: Our Story*** www.lihistory.com *(click on "Colonial Long Island")*

★ ***Virtual Tour of Plimoth Plantation*** pilgrims.net/plymouth/vtour

★ ***Plimoth Plantation*** www.plimoth.org *(click on "Museum")*

Activities on Colonial America

⭐ Discussion Prompts

Use these prompts to stimulate discussion of themes and issues of the colonial period.

★ **Book Reports.** Divide the class into groups and assign each group a fiction title of an appropriate reading level from the bibliography. Members of each group must read their book, discuss it and work together to prepare a book report to share with the class. The report may be presented by one or more representatives of the group and should cover at least these items:

- Title, author and illustrator.
- Summary of plot and main characters.
- What colonial events or issues were most important in the book?
- What did readers learn from the book that could be useful to them now?
- Critical review by the group: Did readers like the book? Why or why not?
- Does the group recommend the book to other readers?

★ **Religious Freedom.** Books on Colonial America tell us that many people came to the New World from Europe seeking freedom to worship as they saw fit. Ask students to respond to these questions, based on their reading. Encourage them to give examples from the books when possible.

- What European religious restrictions were the colonists trying to escape?
- Did they succeed in finding religious freedom in America?
- Did the experience of religious repression in Europe cause the colonists to show more tolerance for people whose beliefs were different from theirs? Did they try to protect the freedom of worship of other Christian groups? Of Native Americans? Of African slaves?
- What were other reasons, besides a desire for religious freedom, that Europeans came to the New World?

★ **Getting the Job Done.** Many of the original British colonists were wealthy or prominent members of British society who were not used to heavy labor or skilled in crafts or trades. How did they manage to build forts and settlements, feed the people and develop profitable businesses? Who taught them survival skills, and how did they meet the need for heavy labor? Make sure that you include the use of indentured servants and slaves in your discussion. Again, use examples from the stories.

★ **Salem Witch Trials.** With the class, review the book *Tituba* to stimulate discussion of the Salem witch trials of 1692–93. These questions might help.

- How did the fear and craziness of the Salem witch trials begin?
- Why do you think so many people in Salem Village believed in witches?
- People sometimes feel fear and become superstitious about things they don't understand. Why were these people so superstitious? What kinds of unexplained things were happening around them that made them fearful?
- Why do you think some of the people accused of witchcraft confessed?
- At least 19 people were executed or died as a result of being accused of witchcraft and we remember it now as a shameful event in our national history. What lessons can we learn from these tragic events that will help us to be more reasonable and fair today and in the future?

⭐ Games

★ **Colonial Figures Matching Game.** Have students match the names of well-known figures from Colonial America to their roles or identities. See reproducible handout on page 16.

★ **Quoits.** A precursor to horseshoes, this game goes back more than 2000 years. It was a favorite among colonial children and adults. The game is best played outside on a flat, grassy surface, but a little creative adaptation could make it a fun break in the classroom.

To make the game, you will need:

> about 75 inches of rope or clothesline
> ruler or tape measure
> scissors
> masking tape
> red and black marking pens
> 18- to 20-inch wooden stake or stick

- Stretch out the rope and cut a 15-inch piece. Repeat three more times to make four 15-inch pieces of rope. Set the remaining rope aside.

- Loop one piece of rope into a circle. Touch the ends together and wrap masking tape several times around where they join. Add more tape if necessary to form a ring that won't fall apart when you toss it. Repeat with the other three lengths of rope.

close the circle and
join with tape

- Color the masking tape on each quoit, making two red and two black.

- Shove the stake or stick firmly into the ground. About 20 feet from the stake, lay the remaining piece of rope on the ground so that it is crossways to the stake. This is the tossing line—the line each player stands behind to toss the quoits.

- Tip the stake a little in the direction of the tossing line.

- Stand at the tossing line and practice tossing quoits. Move the tossing line forward or back from the stake until you have a distance that makes it hard to score a ringer, but not impossible. Players must not step over the line when tossing their quoits.

To play the game:

- Each player, or team, gets two quoits of the same color, either red or black.

- The first player, or team, tosses their quoits from behind the line. They aim at the stake. The second player, or team, follows with two tosses.

To score:

- When a quoit encircles the stake it's called a ringer. The player or team scores 2 points.

- If a player's quoit is closer to the stake than his opponent's, he scores 1 point.

- If a player throws a ringer and her opponent tops it, neither side scores.

- The first player or team to score 21 points wins.

★ **Native American Stick Toss.** Native Americans enjoyed games of chance as well as games of skill. This game, which was played in some form by many North American Indian tribes, may have involved wagers and gambling. It can be enjoyed (without the gambling element) as a special activity or learning center in the classroom. To make the game, you will need:

> 4 craft sticks or tongue depressors
>
> red, yellow and black fine-tip marking pens or felt-tip pens
>
> 15 counting sticks, such as twigs or pencils
>
> 2, 3 or 4 players

- Use the pens to color the four craft sticks as shown. ***Note:*** *Only the rain stick has markings on the back. The lightning, sun and four directions sticks are blank on the back sides.*

Stick 1 – Lightning

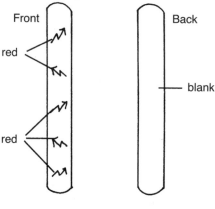

Stick 2 – Sun

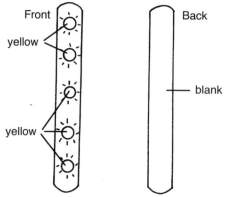

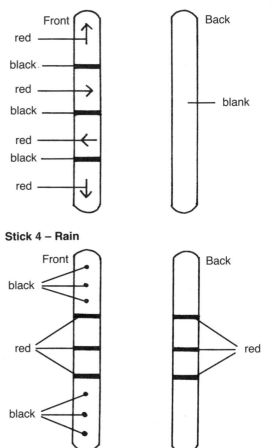

Stick 3 – Four Directions

Front
- red
- black
- red
- black
- red
- black
- red

Back
- blank

Stick 4 – Rain

Front
- black
- red
- black

Back
- red

To play:

- The players sit facing one another. (If four people are playing, form teams of two.) Place the 15 counting sticks off to one side.

- The first player picks up the four craft sticks. Using just the fingertips of one hand, she holds the sticks in a bunch by their tops, then gently tosses them in the air so that they land on the playing surface between the players.

- The player who tosses the sticks scores points according to which sides of the sticks are facing up. The scoring is:

  Front side of four directions: 4 points

  Front side of rain: 3 points

  Front side of lightning: 1 point

  Front side of sun: 1 point

  Back side of lightning, sun, or four directions: 0 points each

  Back side of rain: cancels out entire score for that toss

- After the player tosses, she picks up the number of counting sticks equal to her

score. For example, if her toss was rain, lightning, blank, blank, her score would be 4 points. She would then take 4 counting sticks from the pile. If she tossed the back side of rain, however, her score would be canceled and her turn would be over.

- As long as player one continues to score, she keeps tossing. As soon as she tosses the back side of rain, it is the next player's turn.

- When all 15 counting sticks have been removed from the pile, the player scoring points takes the correct number of counting sticks from the other player's or team's pile.

To win:

- The game officially ends when one player has all 15 counting sticks, but it seldom works that way. The game can continue for a long time, so the players usually decide when the game ends. In that case, the player with the most counting sticks wins.

★ Artistic/Creative Expressions

★ **Dramatic Presentations.** Divide students into several small groups and assign each to prepare a dramatic presentation of a scene from one of the books in this chapter. Students will need to assign roles; create appropriate dialogue, props and actions; and rehearse and present their scene to the class. Costumes would enhance the fun, creativity and effectiveness of the exercise. In planning costumes, you might find *18th Century Clothing,* a title in Kalman's Historic Communities series, helpful. Interesting scenes might include the courtroom scene in chapter 14 of *The 13th Floor;* the meeting of Connecticut leaders with Sir Edmund Andros near the end of *The Secret of Sachem's Tree,* in which the Charter disappears; or the scene in chapter one of *The Double Life of Pocahontas,* in which Pocahontas saves the life of John Smith, thus adopting him into her Powhatan family.

★ **Journal Writing.** Using *Amos Fortune,* Christopher Sears of *Stranded at Plimoth Plantation* or William from *Saturnalia* as inspiration, imagine yourself as someone recently delivered into slavery or indentured servitude. Write a journal entry describing the day you arrived in your new home and workplace.

★ **Shadowgraphs or Silhouettes.** Colonists sometimes decorated their homes with silhouette portraits, which were personal, attractive and inexpensive. Divide students into pairs and have them create silhouettes of each other as follows:

- Find the darkest room possible for drawing the silhouettes.

- Tape a large sheet of white paper to the wall for each portrait.

- Have the subject sit sideways on a chair in front of the paper so his or her profile faces the artist.

- Aim a flashlight at the subject's head to cast a shadow image on the white paper behind. You may have to adjust the positions of the paper, subject and flashlight until you see a clear profile shadow. Secure the flashlight in place by setting it on a table or other surface, propped up as needed.

- Carefully trace around the shadow profile down to the shoulder, including every small detail. Bits of hair out of place or natural irregularities of the nose or forehead are what make these works of art interesting and personal!

- Cut out the silhouette very carefully. For a white on black silhouette, mount the cutout on black paper. To make the more traditional black on white silhouette, cut the silhouette from inside the image and mount the background white paper on black paper, or retrace and cut the image on black paper and mount it on white.

★ **A Family to Follow.** This activity could be used for any chapter of the book, but might be most interesting if begun with this chapter and built on for each succeeding chapter. It could be assigned as an individual, small group or whole class project. Based on the reading, have students create a fictional character, preferably about their age. Develop this character by placing him or her in the context of a family and everyday life in a particular time and place during the period. Then create a story about a day or a week in the character's life. The story might stress ordinary daily activities like work, play or school; might describe a holiday or special event in the character's life; or might show the character involved in some historical event from the period. It might take the form of a short story, poem, song or play. It should be presented with a visual component, e.g., a portrait of the character appropriately costumed. In future chapters, this character's descendants will be revisited through similar activities. Offer suggestions as needed, but let students take initiative and be as creative as their abilities allow.

★ **Creative Response.** Have students select a favorite character from the books listed in this chapter, then create a poem, song, dance or work of visual art about some part of that character's life.

Practical Crafts

★ **Indian Pudding.** Arrange for use of a school kitchen or home economics room and have students cook this popular colonial dessert. The pudding is a sweetened version of the corn pudding mentioned so often as a diet staple in this chapter's books. Work in groups of 6–8 so each group can taste the results of its own efforts.

- Preheat the oven to 300° F.

- Grease a small baking dish with butter or margarine.

- In a medium saucepan, blend 2½ cups milk and ¾ cup cornmeal over medium heat. Cook until thickened, stirring often.

- In a small bowl, lightly beat 2 eggs. Gradually add the eggs to the hot mixture, stirring constantly, until blended.

- Stir in ½ cup molasses and ¼ teaspoon salt.

- Remove the mixture from the heat and pour it into the baking dish.

- Bake for 45 minutes. Serve warm.

★ **Samplers.** Women in colonial days had to know how to sew. Woven cloth was scarce and it was the job of women and girls in the family to make sure that clothes were well made and well mended and that scrap fabric was reused in quilts or rugs. Sewing samplers became a basic part of a girl's education. As a girl practiced her stitches, she could also learn the alphabet, practice her numbers and demonstrate her virtue by embroidering prayers, poems or Bible verses. Invite students to learn about the education of colonial girls and to try their hand at one of the sampler projects in *A Sampler View of Colonial Life with Projects Kids Can Make*. Students might enjoy trying a computer version of a sampler or including poems and sayings that express their personalities. While stitching on fabric is more authentic, drawing and coloring sampler designs on paper will get the idea across.

★ **Dried Fruit.** The closest things colonial families had to refrigerators were root cellars or simple chests they could lower into nearby creeks. So preserving foods to last from harvest time through the winter was a matter of survival. Dried fruit provided nourishment and a tasty treat in the bleak cold of January. Dried apples were used to make pies and ground, dried "berry dust" was used to flavor soups and stews. Have students try their hands at drying fruits in the classroom, following these directions:

- Peel and core apples and cut them into ½-inch slices. String the apple rings on a dowel or pole and hang them in the sunniest part of the room.

- Spread whole blueberries, blackberries or raspberries on a sheet of paper towel placed over a drying rack so that the air circulates around them. Place them, too, where they will catch the sunshine.

- Leave the fruit until it turns brown and rubbery. Then enjoy!

Research Projects

Try these opportunities to explore Colonial America as individual or small group projects, or involve the whole class.

★ **Timeline of Colonial America.** Create a timeline covering major events of the period. Include such things as the establishment of the first European settlements, the Pilgrims' first Thanksgiving, "King Philip's war," major battles of the French and Indian Wars, Bacon's Rebellion, the Salem witch trials, etc. You might assign each student to "nominate" one event for the timeline and to justify the nomination in terms of its historical importance. Consider drawing your timeline on a large roll of paper, then display it in a school hallway. You might add to the timeline as you go through each chapter in this book, eventually producing a truly impressive visual

summary of U.S. history from 1600 to 1970.

★ **Mapping the New World.** Using *The New Americans* and other sources, have students create maps showing one of these things:

- Names and locations of the major Native American groups in the eastern part of the continent in the early 1600s.

- Areas claimed by various European colonial powers in the late 1600s.

- Established trade routes among the New World colonies, Europe, the Caribbean and Africa in the late 1600s, as well as what cargo was carried from point to point.

★ **Model Making.** Using *Stranded at Plimoth Plantation, The New Americans* and other sources, invite students to study and make models of man-made structures from colonial days. Younger students might create replicas of Native American or colonial homes, or birch bark or dugout canoes. More ambitious or older students might make models of ships that brought Europeans to the New World, or even of whole Native American villages or colonial settlements. Models could be made of paper, wood, clay or a variety of other common craft materials. Invite students to share their models and explain both how the original structures were made and how their models were created.

★ **Then and Now.** Have students choose a favorite character from their reading, preferably one close to their age. Students will use their compare and contrast skills to complete the Venn diagram on the reproducible worksheet on page 17. Discuss their findings and conclusions.

★ **My Most Interesting Character.** Assign students to choose a real life character from Colonial America who interests them, and have them learn all they can about that person's life. Students will write a report on that person to share with the class. In addition to references from bibliography titles, you might refer students to other sources such as the Colonial Leaders series mentioned in the chapter introduction, Colonial America Biographies from Gale or the biography section of the school media center or local public library.

Colonial Figures Matching Game

Draw a line from the names of the well-known figures from Colonial America in the first column to their roles or identities in the second column.

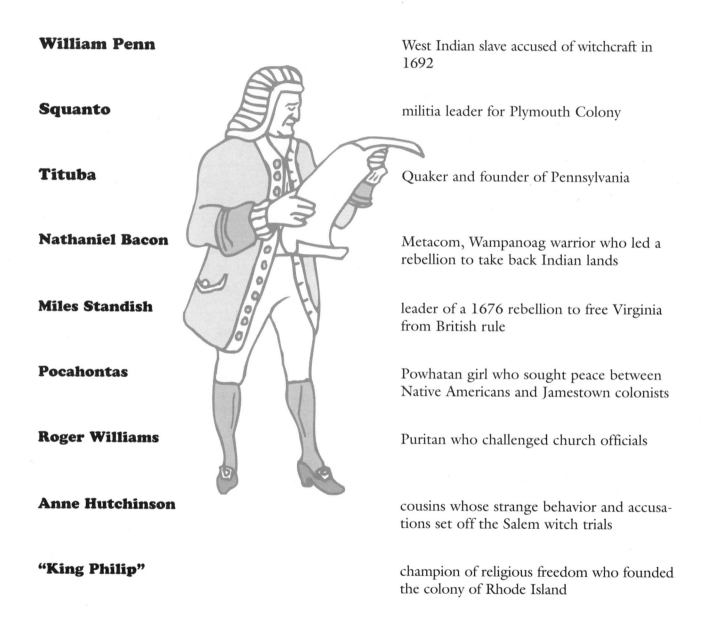

William Penn

Squanto

Tituba

Nathaniel Bacon

Miles Standish

Pocahontas

Roger Williams

Anne Hutchinson

"King Philip"

Elizabeth Parris and Abigail Williams

West Indian slave accused of witchcraft in 1692

militia leader for Plymouth Colony

Quaker and founder of Pennsylvania

Metacom, Wampanoag warrior who led a rebellion to take back Indian lands

leader of a 1676 rebellion to free Virginia from British rule

Powhatan girl who sought peace between Native Americans and Jamestown colonists

Puritan who challenged church officials

cousins whose strange behavior and accusations set off the Salem witch trials

champion of religious freedom who founded the colony of Rhode Island

Pawtuxet Indian who helped the Plymouth Colony survive

Then and Now

Instructions

1. Choose a favorite character from your reading for this chapter. For this exercise, it's better to choose a character not too far from your own age.

2. Think about how your character's life was similar to your life and how it was different. Consider things like family life, school, work, friends and recreation. You might want to make some notes to help you organize your thoughts.

3. Complete the Venn diagram below, recording details about your life in the left circle and details about your character's life in the right circle. List things that are similar in the area that is part of both circles.

Your Life   **Your Character's Life**

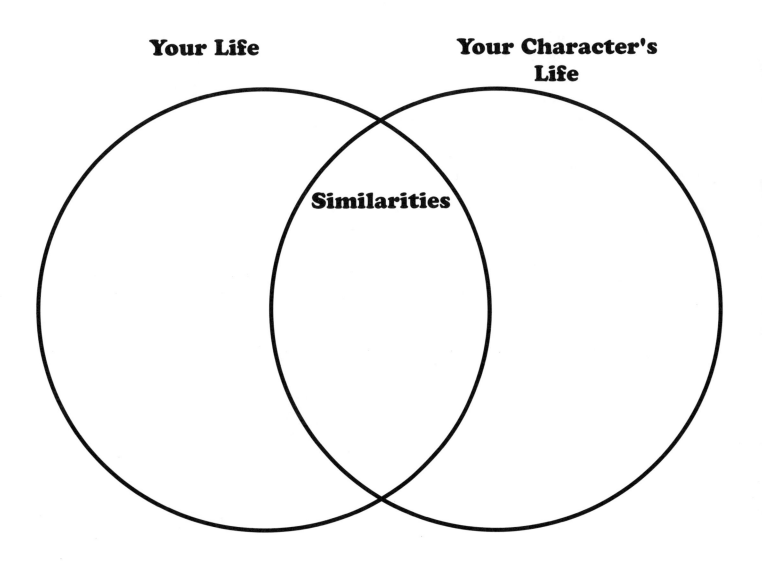

Similarities

The Revolutionary War and the Founding of a Nation

Our nation was born out of intense and youthful passions, with many parallels to the process of adolescents breaking away from parental control and claiming the right to live their own lives. A growing awareness of different needs, resources and circumstances from "the mother country," a sense of unjust and excessive control from the parent country and the idealism of a grand destiny to fulfill—all of these things mirror the process of establishing oneself as an independent adult. In the struggle to deal with the realities of independence and the need to organize in new ways we see more parallels to the maturing process of individuals. Fortunately, most individuals don't have to go through a bloody war or integrate 13 very diverse parts of themselves to accomplish their goals as did the emerging United States of America!

We see, in this brief but dramatic and turbulent period in our history (1775–1787), an intoxicating and devastating mix of fierce loyalties, uncompromising principles, glorious heroism, deep disappointment, terrible losses and suffering, inspired rhetoric and deft statesmanship. The world was truly watching as our ancestors began this flawed but exciting and ongoing experiment in representative democracy.

Some themes of this period to explore through literature include:

★ Choosing sides: Who fought and for what?

★ Revolution or civil war?

★ Heroes and leaders.

★ United we stand; divided we fall.

★ Making our own rules: Adopting the Constitution.

★ The ideal of freedom, but from what and for whom?

Some additional series that might enrich your exploration include:

★ Clothing, Costumes and Uniforms throughout American History by Allison Stark Draper. PowerKids Press. K–4. *Note: These easy readers are intended for younger students, but good illustrations and information may make them useful for older students.*

★ Daughters of Liberty by Elizabeth Massie. Pocket Books. 4–6.

★ Young Founders by Elizabeth Massie. Tom Doherty Associates. 6–8.

Resources on the Revolutionary War and the Founding of a Nation

★ Fiction

★ **The Arrow Over the Door** by Joseph Bruchac. Dial Books for Young Readers, 1998. 4–8. Based on an actual event, this brief novel describes an encounter between a small Abenaki party, scouting for King George, and a meetinghouse full of Quakers. Chapters alternate voices between Stands Straight, an Abenaki youth, and Samuel, a Quaker boy, both of whom have reason to mistrust the other, but hesitate to fight. The encounter eases Samuel's distress about his family's pacifist beliefs and convinces the Indians not to aid the British against Americans.

★ **Buttons for General Washington** by Peter and Connie Roop. Carolrhoda Books, 1986. 4–5. In easy reader format, the Roops relate an adventure of child spy John Darragh who, with his Quaker family, smuggled coded messages to General Washington hidden in the buttons of John's coat. While the incident is fictional, the unlikely spy family was real. A good story to fire the imaginations of young students.

★ **Cast Two Shadows: The American Revolution in the South** by Ann Rinaldi. Harcourt, 1998. 7–8. War has hit the Whitaker family hard. Caroline's father is imprisoned as a rebel; her brother fights for the British; her sister is dallying with the British officer in charge of their commandeered home; and Caroline has just learned that her mulatto mother, whom she thought was dead, was sold into slavery in the West Indies. In this complex but fast-paced novel, Caroline must deal with some of the most distressing issues of the time and find the strength and resourcefulness to endure and do what must be done. An interesting look at how the war was different in the southern colonies.

★ **George Washington's Socks** by Elvira Woodruff. Scholastic, 1993. 4–6. In this time-travel story, Matt and his Adventure Club buddies, along with his little sister, are whirled away from their Nebraska neighborhood camp-out to the icy Delaware River at Christmas 1776. Their encounter with General Washington and his troops in the midst of carrying out their surprise attacks at Princeton and Trenton creates real dangers and firsthand learning for these likable, contemporary children.

★ **The Hatmaker's Sign: A Story by Benjamin Franklin** retold by Candace Fleming. Orchard Books, 1998. 4–6. Franklin uses this clever parable to ease Thomas Jefferson's wounded pride when his "perfect" draft of the Declaration of Independence is "mutilated" by the Continental Congress. A worthy story in its own right, in context it sheds light on the characters of both Franklin and Jefferson.

★ **Johnny Tremain** by Esther Forbes. Houghton Mifflin, 1998. 5–8. Newbery Medal Book. In this classic title, Johnny Tremain, apprentice silversmith turned Son of Liberty, aids the Sons in the events leading up to "the shot heard 'round the world" as messenger and errand boy. A sensitive and rousing story that shows both the perceived glory and the actual suffering of war through the experiences of a compelling, believable protagonist.

★ **The Keeping Room** by Anna Myers. Puffin Books, 1999. 4–7. Thirteen-year-old Joey Kershaw is left to protect home and family when his father goes to fight with the Rebel army. British troops commandeer the Kershaw home as their headquarters, and Joey witnesses inhuman brutality by British soldiers which he vows to avenge. Well-drawn characters and a riveting plot draw the reader into Joey's experiences of horror and great kindness on both sides of the conflict, and lend credibility to the changes he perceives in himself.

★ **Moon of Two Dark Horses** by Sally M. Keehn. Philomel Books, 1995. 6–8. Delaware Indian youth Coshmoo and white settler Daniel are best friends. As the Revolutionary War encroaches on their peaceful lives, they long to find a way to protect their friendship, their families and their homes from its ravages. But Daniel's farm is destroyed and the neutral Delaware tribe is dragged into the fray. This powerful story portrays the staggering costs and innocent victims of war.

★ **My Brother Sam is Dead** by James Lincoln Collier and Christopher Collier. Scholastic, 1997. 5–8. Newbery Honor Book. Tim doesn't care much about politics or the grow-

ing movement for independence from England. They seem to have nothing to do with him. But his impetuous brother Sam runs off to join the Revolutionary Army and his father can't abide the thought of treason against the king. Sam is caught in the middle and the confusion, danger, violence, loss and bewilderment that enter his life are shared with painful honesty and realism.

★ ***The Riddle of Penncroft Farm*** by Dorothea Jensen. Harcourt, 2001. 5–8. Lars hates being uprooted from his life in Minnesota to move to the family farm in Pennsylvania. But friendship with his mischievous great-aunt and visits from the ghost of a revolutionary ancestor capture his imagination and instill in him a love for Penncroft Farm and a new interest in history. A first-rate, fast-moving ghost story with lots of battle action.

★ ***1787: A Novel*** by Joan Anderson. Harcourt, Brace, Jovanovich, 1987. 6–8. Jared hopes to spend his last summer before college enjoying freedom and friends and courting Hetty Morris. But it's 1787 in Philadelphia and Jared's uncle has other plans for him. As an aide to James Madison, Jared is swept into the drama of the Constitutional Congress, which immerses him in fascinating characters, upsetting intrigue and serious issues facing the emerging nation. A good, digestible look at the complex social and personal issues of representation, racism and classism that we still struggle with today.

★ ***Toliver's Secret*** by Esther Wood Brady. Random House, 1993. 4–6. Ten-year-old Ellen's life has been turned upside down by the war and she's afraid of everything but the warmth of the kitchen. When her grandfather sprains his ankle, he needs her to undertake a dangerous journey delivering a secret message for General Washington. Frightened and dressed as a boy, Ellen embarks on what becomes a series of near-disasters that could get her grandfather hanged as a spy. Yet she perseveres out of love for him and discovers a strong, courageous side of herself. Good human and period drama.

★ ***War Comes to Willy Freeman*** by James Lincoln Collier and Christopher Collier. Dell, 1987. 6–8. Not for the squeamish, this is a distressing story of 13-year-old Wilhelmina (Willy), a free black girl whose father dies fighting for independence and whose mother is taken by the British. On her own and disguised

as a boy, Willy tries to find her mother and make her way in a world in which she is, clearly, "at the bottom of the pile." Her character and courage are as inspiring as the story is upsetting. ***Note:*** *Use of the words "nigger" and "slut," while accurate in historical context, may call for some discussion and discretion.*

Nonfiction

★ ***African Americans and the Revolutionary War*** by Judith E. Harper. Child's World, 2001. 4–8. Harper introduces us to the conditions of African Americans in America before, during and after the Revolutionary War. While telling the overall story she focuses on several individuals who distinguished themselves in a variety of ways. Appealing, well-illustrated picture book format.

★ ***Betsy Ross*** by Alexandra Wallner. Holiday House, 1994. 4–5. This richly illustrated picture book conveys a sense of the complex life of Betsy Ross, reputed creator of the first American flag. Ross challenged her Quaker family by marrying outside the faith and making ammunition for the Revolutionary Army. An author's note explains the uncertain origins of the flag story, which doesn't diminish this introduction to a courageous, independent revolutionary woman.

★ ***Book of the American Revolution*** by Howard Egger-Bovet and Marlene Smith-Baranzini. Little, Brown, 1994. 4–8. This Brown Paper School USKids History title is packed with stories, speeches, cartoons, games and activities that explore many sides of the question of who should own and rule over North America, as they were understood in colonial and revolutionary times.

★ ***Crossing the Delaware: A History in Many Voices*** by Louise Peacock. Atheneum Books for Young Readers, 1998. 4–8. Peacock uses a variety of voices to share the dire circumstances and desperation that prompted General Washington to order his ragged, starving, exhausted troops across the Delaware River on Christmas night, 1776. His unexpected surprise attack and unlikely victory prevented the Revolutionary War from being lost almost before it began.

★ ***The Midnight Ride of Paul Revere*** by Henry Wadsworth Longfellow. National Geographic Society, 2002. 4–8. Longfellow's stirring poem finds new life paired with Jeffrey Thompson's spectacular illustrations. Any student with a pulse will find it quickened to the galloping hoofbeat rhythm of this read-aloud masterpiece.

★ *A More Perfect Union: The Story of Our Constitution* by Betsy and Giulio Maestro. William Morrow & Co., 1991. 4–8. In concise and insightful style, the Maestros summarize the process that resulted in the writing and ratifying of our Constitution and the Bill of Rights. An excellent overview with informative appendixes for introducing, reviewing or stimulating further study.

★ *Phoebe the Spy* by Judith Berry Griffin. Scholastic, 1989. 3–6. Thirteen-year-old Phoebe, daughter of free black tavern keeper Samuel Fraunces, finds herself ensconced in General Washington's residence as a spy, trying to uncover a rumored plot on the General's life. This true story raises issues of child spies and of the irony of blacks fighting for the limited freedoms envisioned by the slaveholding leaders of the Revolution.

★ *Songs and Stories from the American Revolution* by Jerry Silverman. Millbrook Press, 1994. 4–8. Ten Revolutionary War songs are featured in this attractive, well-illustrated book. Accompanying each song is substantial narrative that addresses both the historical events and interesting specifics of melody and lyrics. You might enlist a vocal music teacher to help students prepare songs for performance at a school assembly.

★ *Will You Sign Here, John Hancock?* by Jean Fritz. Putnam, 1997. 4–6. In witty and accessible style, Fritz sketches Hancock as a likable but spoiled "rich kid," motivated in equal parts by sincere devotion to the cause of independence and a desire to be the center of attention. In contrast to the tone of reverence that characterizes many stories of the founding fathers, this very human portrait brings the events, and the people who participated in them, to life in ways to which students might relate.

Other Media

★ *Ben and Me* based on the novel by Robert Lawson. Walt Disney Home Video, 1989 (videocassette, 25 minutes). 4–5. Younger students will enjoy this clever version of the life and accomplishments of Ben Franklin, told by Amos the mouse who (according to Amos) served as Ben's muse, mentor and closest companion from the invention of the Franklin stove through Franklin's 81st birthday. Full of wit, humor and Franklin's famous maxims.

★ *The Fighting Ground* by Avi. Recorded Books, 1994 (three audiocassettes). 6–8. Scott O'Dell Historical Fiction Award Book. George Guidall narrates this gripping, action-packed story of 24 hours in the life of 13-year-old Jonathan, who dreams of being a soldier in the Revolutionary War. Jonathan runs off to join the fighting, but his dreams of glory fade as he is involved in a skirmish, is taken prisoner, escapes and faces a dilemma when asked to lure his captors to their death. There is no romanticizing the brutal, grinding personal realities of war.

Web sites

★ *Declaration of Independence* www.surfnetkids.com/declaration.htm

★ *History Central's American Revolution* www.multied.com/revolt

★ *Introduction to Uniforms of the American Army* www.walika.com/sr/uniforms/uniforms.htm

★ *ThinkQuest's The Revolutionary War: A Journey Towards Freedom* library.thinkquest.org/10966/index.html

★ *ThinkQuest's A Roadmap to the U.S. Constitution* library.thinkquest.org/11572

Activities on the Revolutionary War and the Founding of a Nation

★ Discussion Prompts

Use these prompts to stimulate discussion of themes and issues of the American Revolution.

★ **Standing Up For Your Rights.** Many colonists increasingly saw themselves as "Americans," a separate people with separate needs and concerns, being unfairly controlled by England. When they revolted and adopted the Declaration of Independence, they were standing up for what they believed to be their rights. Lead a discussion on the idea of standing up for your rights, using these prompts.

- What is a "right?" How is it different from a "privilege?"

- What rights does the Declaration of Independence claim are deserved by all people?

- When is a right worth fighting for?

- What rights were the colonists fighting for in the Revolutionary War?

- Do all Americans enjoy the rights today that were fought for in the Revolution and that are promised in the Declaration of Independence and the Constitution?

★ **Round Robin Issues for Older Students.** Divide the class into four groups. Assign group one to read *My Brother Sam is Dead,* group two *Cast Two Shadows,* group three *War Comes to Willy Freeman* and group four *The Keeping Room.* Encourage students to read carefully, paying special attention to issues and concerns of the times addressed in the books. After the reading, regroup according to the plan below and have the combined groups discuss the issues indicated. Each paired discussion group should choose a reporter to take notes for a brief summary to the rest of the class at the end of the discussions. Discussions may be brief—perhaps 15 minutes per grouping. This "round robin" format allows students to come away with a sense of issues of the day and their impact on the people who lived with them.

Note: Be sure to review the annotations and consider content and reading levels when assigning these titles.

- Groups one and two should discuss why some people called the American Revolution a civil war. What is a civil war? What happens to families and communities when members find themselves on opposite sides of an armed struggle? Refer to chapter one of *My Brother Sam* and parts of chapters five and ten of *Cast Two Shadows.*

- At the same time, groups three and four should describe, compare and contrast the main characters in their books, Willy and Joey. Their lives and experiences seem very different. Still, they would have much to learn from each other. Have students imagine a meeting between these characters, and discuss what they might want to say to one another.

- Now rearrange groups. Groups two and three should discuss the involvement and hopes of African Americans in the war. What were black slaves promised by each side, and what were they actually given? Have students note parts of chapters one and five to eight in *War Comes to Willy Freeman,* and parts of chapters one and five in *Cast Two Shadows* for ideas.

- At the same time, groups one and four should compare the female characters in their books. Look especially at Tim's mother and Betsy in *My Brother Sam is Dead,* and at Mother and Mary in *The Keeping Room.* Find passages in the books that describe these characters, and discuss how they were alike and different. What roles did these girls and women play in the war? What opinions did they hold about the war, and how did they act on their convictions? How were they limited in their opportunities to act by being female?

- Regroup one last time. Groups one and three should discuss the violence and atrocities practiced by both sides during the Revolutionary War. The most disturbing scenes in these books (in chapter two of *War Comes to Willy Freeman* and the last half of chapter X in *My Brother Sam is Dead*) happen to feature brutality by British soldiers. Be sure students remember that it was American sympathizers who terrorized Tim and his father and captured Tim's father. Is it possible to have a war without excessive and arbitrary brutality? What do you think happens to young people who witness such horrible violence? Are they changed forever? Do you think, as Tim does at the end of *My Brother Sam is Dead,* that there might have been another way to achieve independence from England?

- Groups two and four should discuss their main characters' common experiences of having their homes commandeered by the enemy and awakening to the condition of slaves in the South. Joey, who has lived a privileged life served by slaves and whose father feels that slavery "fits the order of things," grows closer to Cato and learns about his life in *The Keeping Room.* He begins to question the rightness of slavery. See especially chapters three and twelve. Caroline, born to a slave but adopted into the wealthy home of her white father, is made a servant in her own home in *Cast Two Shadows.* She bonds with her slave grandmother and awakens to the plight of slaves during the occupation of Tory soldiers. See chapter fifteen. What do these characters learn about life in slavery? How might these characters use what they learn to help make things better for future generations?

- Reassemble the class as a whole, and have each group reporter present highlights from the discussion.

Games

★ **Acrostic Puzzle.** An acrostic is a word puzzle that can be read up and down as well as across. The letters of a word or name, written vertically, are used in other words or phrases written horizontally to create a meaningful composition. Acrostics were popular in colonial and revolutionary days. We learn in *Book of the American Revolution* (p. 56) that an uncle of Benjamin Franklin wrote an acrostic for young Ben, based on his name, to guide his behavior. Share that example or create one together as a class. Then have students write their own acrostic compositions, based on their names and describing themselves, their qualities and their dreams or goals. Use the worksheet on page 26.

★ **Spy Codes.** Review *Buttons for General Washington* with the class. You will also find information about Revolutionary War spies and spy codes in *Book of the American Revolution.* Both the British and the Americans used spies and coded messages to try to gain advantage over the enemy. Some secret messages were shared in foreign languages; some were written with missing letters or with invisible ink that required the reader to know how to make the message reappear. Many spies, like the Darragh family, relied on codes of their own making to convey their messages. Have students create coded messages, following the directions below.

- Divide the class into two groups. Assign one group to use a cipher and the other group to use a book code to create secret messages.

- Have each group create the message they want to deliver, or assign each group a message related to something happening in the classroom. Just for fun, you might use something like this: "The group that decodes its secret message fastest gets an extra five minutes of recess!"

- The cipher group will create its own cipher code, replacing each letter of the alphabet with a different letter. For example, in their cipher, "C" might stand for "X," "T" for "J," "A" for "S," etc. Ciphers that follow a predictable pattern are easier to "crack;" those assigned randomly are much harder. Once the cipher is created, the group will rewrite the message in their code.

- The book code group will work from a particular book available in the classroom, translating each word in their message into a code of three numbers that stand for the page, the line and then the word on that line that they are disguising. For example, if the word you wanted to translate is "enemy," and you use this book as your reference, you could write it as "23, 14, 1."

- Once the messages are coded, the groups will swap secret messages and try to break the code. **Note:** *The book code group will have to be a bit sneaky, because if the cipher group sees what book they are referencing, their message will be very easy to decode. Remember, part of the trick of book codes is that only the sender and the receiver know what the book is and have copies of it handy.*

★ Artistic/Creative Expressions

★ **"Franklinisms."** Ben Franklin was famous for his clever, often funny and wise sayings about life, some of which you'll find in *Ben and Me.* Some famous "Franklinisms" are "A penny saved is a penny earned," "Waste not, want not" and "Early to bed and early to rise, makes a man healthy, wealthy and wise." Have students make up their own "Franklinisms" to post around the classroom.

★ **Designing a Flag.** Review *Betsy Ross* with the class, and talk about the symbolism of the design of the first American flag. Then have students create their own flag—either individual flags to represent themselves or a single flag for the classroom. Have students explain why their flag is designed as it is.

★ *Crossing the Delaware* **Dramatic Reading.** Stage a reader's theater style performance of this dramatic book, using two main narrators and a variety of readers to tell the story. Costumes, music and appropriate visuals could make a stunning presentation for a school assembly.

★ **A Family to Follow.** Building on the activity with the same title in chapter one, invite students to imagine moving forward in time to the Revolutionary War era. What has happened to your character's family since then? Create a new character that is descended from the original character and go through similar steps to tell a story about this period. Place the new character solidly in time and place and explain his or her relationship to the original character. You might enrich this ongoing activity by beginning a fictional family tree, starting with your original character and showing the generations to the time of your new character.

★ Practical Crafts

★ **Classroom Quilt.** Woven fabric was still scarce and expensive during this time, and most Americans learned to make full use of every bit they had. A creative way to use scraps of cloth from worn-out clothing was in patchwork quilts. While quilting has become an art and it is unrealistic to expect a class to produce a fine quilt, students can get a taste of the process by making a classroom quilt from paper. Have each student create an origi-

nal design using crayons, markers or paint on eight-inch squares of white paper. Invite students to research traditional quilt patterns from the period while designing their squares. Then arrange the squares in an attractive pattern on a wall of the classroom for a beautiful reflection of the Revolutionary War era.

★ **Classic Fireplace Stew.** In *My Brother Sam is Dead,* Tim's family's tavern always has stew simmering in the fireplace. Arrange for use of a school kitchen or home economics room and have students cook this hearty standard fare from the period. Work in groups of six to eight students, so each group can enjoy its own batch. You'll need:

> 1½ pounds beef stew meat
>
> 1 large onion, chopped
>
> 2 celery stalks, chopped
>
> 1 medium turnip, chopped
>
> 4 potatoes, chopped
>
> 6 carrots, chopped
>
> Seasonings: A combination of salt, black pepper, parsley, bay leaf, thyme, crushed red pepper and "berry dust" (crushed dried berries), to taste.

• Brown the stew meat and onions in a heavy cooking pot.

• Add 4 cups of water, vegetables and seasonings.

• Simmer 20–30 minutes, until vegetables are tender.

• For a thicker stew add a tablespoon of cornmeal at a time during the last 10 minutes of cooking, until you achieve the desired consistency.

Note: Check for food allergies (including corn).

★ Research Projects

Try these opportunities to explore the Revolutionary War and the founding of the U.S. as individual or small group projects, or involve the whole class.

★ **Revolutionary War Weapons.** Invite interested students to research weapons used by soldiers of the British and American armies during the war. To begin, mention references to the common "Brown Bess" musket and bayonets in both *The Fighting Ground* and *My Brother Sam is Dead*, to the British cannons in *Toliver's Secret* and the "Turtle" submarine invented by David Bushnell in *Book of the American Revolution*. Students should report their findings to the class, with illustrations and explanations as appropriate. An Internet search might be very useful for this topic.

★ **Major Battles of the Revolutionary War.** Have students choose a particular battle of the war and become amateur experts on the subject. Encourage them to share their knowledge with the class in creative ways, such as a model recreation of the battlefield, a song or a poem.

★ **Signers of the Declaration of Independence.** Have students choose one of the delegates to the Continental Congress that signed the Declaration of Independence. Assign them to learn all they can about their delegate. Use the reproducible worksheet on page 27 to organize the research, but encourage students to go beyond the basics and find interesting stories about their delegate. History Central's American Revolution and the Declaration of Independence Web sites mentioned on page 21 may be useful. Students can share their results based on the worksheets.

Acrostic Puzzle

An acrostic puzzle is a word puzzle that can be read up and down as well as across. The letters of a word or name, written vertically, are used in other words or phrases that are written horizontally to create a meaningful composition. Acrostics were popular during colonial and Revolutionary War days in America.

Here's an example:

John Hancock was
fr **O** m
Massac **H** usetts
vai **N**

a good **H** ost
d **A** ring Patriot
N ot a good sailor
C harming
fam **O** us for his signature
ri **C** h
John Hancoc **K**

Write your own acrostic composition, based on your name, that describes you, your qualities and your dreams or goals.

Signers of the Declaration of Independence

Choose a Continental Congress delegate that signed the Declaration of Independence. Research your delegate, then fill out the worksheet. If you can, try to find an interesting story about your delegate and write it on the back of this worksheet.

My delegate to the Continental Congress is _____ .

What colony was he from? _____

Where did he live? (In what city, or on a farm near what city?) _____

Was he wealthy or poor? How did he make his living? _____

_____

He was _____ years old at the time of the signing of the Declaration of Independence.

Did he have a family at home? Describe. _____

_____

Was he a leader or did he provide a special service to the Congress? Explain._____

_____

_____

I chose this delegate because _____

_____

How did this delegate feel about declaring independence from England? _____

_____

Did he suggest or fight for any particular changes to the wording of the Declaration?

_____

Westward Expansion and Frontier Life

The period of westward expansion and frontier life began before the Revolutionary War and extended beyond the Civil War into the early 1900s. It was a time of incredibly rapid changes on the North American continent and involved one of the largest mass migrations in human history. By the time the U.S. Constitution was adopted, the country had already doubled in size from the original 13 colonies that declared independence from England. By 1853, less than 70 years later, America had expanded its land holdings and increased its population several times over. It reached from the Atlantic to the Pacific and from present-day Canada to present-day Mexico. There were 31 United States of America. People had come from around the world to settle the west, find adventure, run from the law, acquire free land, get rich quick, escape from slavery or simply better their lot.

In 1840, "the West" still meant anything west of Missouri, and most of it was sparsely populated foreign territory. As a nation, we are dazzled by the myths and legends inspired by this "bigger than life" landscape and the accompanying drama and adventure. We must also remember that entire populations were displaced and that long-established ways of life, true wilderness and several species of animals all but disappeared forever, casualties of the concept of Manifest Destiny.

Some themes of this period to explore through literature include:

★ The notion and consequences of Manifest Destiny.

★ Explorers and trailblazers.

★ The Wild West.

★ Gold fever!

★ Connecting a nation: Transportation and communication.

★ Legends, heroes and characters.

★ Joys and hardships of frontier life.

★ Immigrants, old and new.

Some additional series that might enrich your exploration include:

★ The Little House books by Laura Ingalls Wilder. HarperCollins. 4–5.

★ Once Upon America. Puffin Books. 4–6.

★ Orphan Train Adventures by Joan Lowery Nixon. Bantam Doubleday Dell. 5–8.

Resources on Westward Expansion and Frontier Life

Fiction

★ ***Bluestem*** by Frances Arrington. Philomel Books, 2000. 4–7. Not every pioneer could withstand the harsh, endless prairie. In this haunting novel, Mama succumbs to mental illness after the death of two babies and wanders off into the grass ocean, leaving Polly and Jesse to endure and protect their claim until Papa returns. The fear, despair, determination and courage of the young sisters are palpable as they face obstacles no children should have to handle alone.

★ ***The Borning Room*** by Paul Fleischman. Scholastic, 1991. 6–8. An Ohio pioneer girl shares her life, and the great changes she's seen, through memories of events that take place in this room reserved for birth, illness and death. Medical treatments, slavery, the Spiritualist movement and early use of electricity find their way into the parade of images that impact the basic life cycle at the story's core.

★ ***Dragon's Gate*** by Laurence Yep. HarperCollins, 1995. 6–8. Newbery Honor Book. Otter flees trouble in China to join his father and uncle as a laborer building the transcontinental railroad in the Sierra Mountains. He experiences the harsh injustice of conditions for Chinese laborers, has to adjust his image of his idolized uncle to fit reality and proves his own courage and leadership in crisis. Ultimately, Otter finds a goal for his life founded on personal convictions rather than blind tradition.

★ ***Fat Chance, Claude*** by Joan Lowery Nixon. Penguin Putnam Books for Young Readers, 1991. 4–5. Shirley isn't your ordinary pioneer girl. She learns to rope, rustle and fix and isn't interested in finding a husband. Instead, she heads west in her own covered wagon to pan for gold. Along the way she meets Claude and, in spite of their differences, they discover they've each found just the right partner for business and for life. A clever, funny look at frontier courtship.

★ ***Follow the Drinking Gourd*** by Jeanette Winter. Alfred A. Knopf, 1992. 4–8. The famous song that directed runaway slaves along the Underground Railroad to freedom is set in the context of a particular story in this dramatically illustrated picture book. While such journeys didn't always end this happily, the book conveys how the railroad operated, as well as the dangers encountered and the courage and dedication of all involved.

★ ***The Gentleman Outlaw and Me—Eli: A Story of the Old West*** by Mary Downing Hahn. Avon Books, 1997. 5–8. Eliza Yates, disguised as Elijah Bates, flees from unscrupulous relatives to find her father out west. She falls in with a young would-be outlaw seeking to avenge his father's murder. The journey takes the unlikely pair on a roller-coaster ride of good and bad luck, Wild West mining towns, two-bit cons and colorful characters. It's a fun and exciting glimpse of life in the frontier west.

★ ***I Have Heard of a Land*** by Joyce Carol Thomas. HarperCollins, 1999. 4–8. ALSC Notable Children's Book, Coretta Scott King Honor Book. This beautiful, lyrical picture book tells of an African American woman who stakes a claim in Oklahoma during the land rush and farms on her own to make a home for her family. Her hardships, determination and ultimate success add dimension to our picture of "typical American pioneers."

★ ***The Journey Home*** by Isabelle Holland. Scholastic, 1993. 5–8. The dying wish of Maggie and Annie's mother is that they go west on an orphan train to find a new family and a healthier life. They are adopted by a childless couple on the Kansas prairie, where they must deal with prejudices, illnesses and difficult adjustments before they learn to feel at home. Strong-willed, convincing characters make this story engaging and satisfying.

★ ***Mr. Tucket*** by Gary Paulsen. Bantam Doubleday Dell Books for Young Readers, 1995. 5–8. Fourteen-year-old Francis Tucket is abducted from his wagon train by Pawnees. A crusty, one-armed mountain man named Mr. Grimes rescues him. The two share a series of adventures ranging from humorous to tragic and develop a bond of affection and understanding along the way. Francis has to learn fast and grow up in a hurry. This rip-roaring novel is part of Paulsen's series of

Tucket adventures, written with his characteristic finesse.

★ *Night of the Full Moon* by Gloria Whelan. Random House, 1996. 4–5. This advanced reader tells of the friendship between pioneer girl Libby and Potawatomi girl Fawn in Michigan during the summer of 1840. The families are good neighbors and encourage the friendship, but when Libby is caught up in the forced removal of Fawn and her people from their campground, the depth and honor of their bond is tested and proven.

★ *The Prairie Train* by Antoine Ó Flatharta. Crown Publishers, 1999. 4–6. This enchanting picture book combines elements of fantasy with an introduction to the concept of mass immigration to the American West. A young boy named Conor travels from Ireland with his family and immigrants from all over Europe, to ride this train to their new home in San Francisco. Their shared adventure and Conor's dream cause him to look with hope to the future.

★ *Remember My Name* by Sara H. Banks. Roberts Rinehart Publishers, 1993. 4–7. Events culminating in the shameful Trail of Tears are presented in this Council for Indian Education series title. Orphaned 11-year-old Annie goes to live with her wealthy Cherokee uncle, where she befriends his slave girl Righteous and her mother Charity. As the government reneges on promise after promise to the Cherokees, it becomes obvious they will be forcibly removed to make room for white settlers. Uncle William frees his slaves and orchestrates an escape for Annie, Righteous and Charity, while he prepares to accompany his people on their terrible journey. This book challenges stereotypes about the period.

★ *Sarah, Plain and Tall* by Patricia MacLachlan. HarperCollins, 1999. 4–6. Scott O'Dell Historical Fiction Award Book, Newbery Medal Book. This story tells of Caleb and Anna, who need a mother, and of Sarah, the "want-ads" potential bride Papa invites to join their family on the plains. Sarah misses her seaside home, and the awkwardness of trying to form a new family challenges these endearing characters. A gentle story of hope and strength, also adapted into a television movie.

★ *Sing Down the Moon* by Scott O'Dell. Econo-Clad, 1997. 5–8. Newbery Honor Book. Bright Moon seeks to hold onto her courage and the nobility of her people as she is first abducted into slavery and later, after escaping, forcibly removed with her Navajo tribe to the Four Corners area on The Long Walk.

★ *Soon Be Free* by Lois Ruby. Simon & Schuster Books for Young Readers, 2000. 6–8. A mystery unfolds in alternate chapters written from the viewpoints of two teens who live in the same Kansas house, 150 years apart. Dana, the modern teen, tries to discover what secret is hidden in the historic old house, given new life as a bed and breakfast inn, that is valuable enough to cause their first guests to vandalize and steal. James, the 1850s teen, relates his thrilling and distressing adventure guiding runaway slaves to Kansas from the South. The stories converge, leading to an intriguing and satisfying conclusion

★ *Swamp Angel* by Anne Isaacs. Viking Penguin, 1999. 4–8. Caldecott Honor Book. While not as well known as the tales about Pecos Bill or Davy Crockett, these stories of the amazing feats of Angelica Longrider, "the greatest woodswoman in Tennessee," are just as bold, entertaining and satisfyingly true to the tall-tale tradition. Zelinsky's beautiful illustrations complement the witty text to create a delightful picture book.

★ Nonfiction

★ *Brother Eagle, Sister Sky: A Message from Chief Seattle* by Susan Jeffers. Penguin Putnam Books for Young Readers, 2002. 4–8. In Chief Seattle's response to the U.S. Government's request to buy the lands of the Northwest Nations in the 1850s, he eloquently sets forth Native American respect for the sacredness of the land and all life on it. He speaks of concern and warning about how carelessly the land and its inhabitants were treated during America's rush to settle the western lands. Beautiful illustrations make this a likely read-aloud title.

★ *Cowboys* by Stewart Ross. Copper Beech Books, 1995. 4–8. As a Fact or Fiction series title, this slick collection of text and illustrations in thematic two-page spreads traces the origins, history, work, recreation, reality and myths of the legendary cowboys that loom so large in America's imagination. Famous figures of the Wild West, the pony express, the railroad, the rodeo and images of cowboys in modern culture are featured in this entertaining overview.

★ *Daily Life in a Covered Wagon* by Paul Erickson. Puffin Books, 1997. 4–8. In brief, tightly written chapters, we share the four-month wagon train journey of the Larkin family and their fellow "overlanders" along the Oregon Trail in 1853. Interesting detail and captioned photos describe the wagons, landmarks, Native Americans, entertainment, daily routines and dangers of the journey.

★ *Daniel Boone* by Arthur Guiterman. 5–8. This poem, while not available as a stand-alone volume, can be found in several collections including *Wide Open Spaces: American Frontiers* (Perfection Learning, 2001), *The Moon is Shining Bright as Day* edited by Ogden Nash (HarperCollins, 1953) and *Favorite Poems Old and New* edited by Helen Ferris (Doubleday Books for Young Readers, 1957). It eulogizes the legendary hero, whose life and deeds strongly echo the events and spirit of the frontier. The poem lends itself to stimulating research; one of the Research Project activities on page 35 is based on it.

★ *Gold Fever! Tales from the California Gold Rush* by Rosalyn Schanzer. National Geographic Society, 1999. 4–8. Snippets, quotes, anecdotes and lively illustrations of many people involved in the 1848 gold rush explore their motives and experiences, along with the frenzy of this period of mass migration and rapid, dramatic change. Presented with humor and balance, it may engage students and stimulate further research.

★ *Mississippi Mud: Three Prairie Journals* by Ann Turner. HarperCollins, 1997. 4–8. Turner shares the fictional journals, in the form of poems, of three siblings as they leave Kentucky and travel by wagon train to their new home in Oregon. Small details and major events help us see into their experiences and feelings.

★ *A Pioneer Sampler* by Barbara Greenwood. Houghton Mifflin, 1998. 4–8. Everything you ever wanted to know about daily life on a backwoods farm in 1840 in one volume! Concise one- or two-page spreads and sidebars about everything from hunting techniques to holidays are interspersed with vignettes in the lives of the fictional Robertson family and their neighbors. The characters have enough personality to be believable and winning. The book includes recipes, games, craft projects and other activities to bring the pioneer experience to life.

Other Media

★ *Johnny Appleseed* retold by Garrison Keillor. Rabbit Ears Productions, 1992 (videocassette, 30 minutes). 4–8. Through the first half of the 1800s this folk hero wandered alone through Pennsylvania, Ohio, Indiana and Illinois planting and tending apple trees as settlers moved west. This quirky telling of his story gives more depth than most, alluding to his pre-nomadic past and taking him to his peaceful, fanciful death.

★ *The Oregon Trail, 4th Edition.* The Learning Company, 1999 (three interactive CDs). 5–8. Players of this exciting interactive game simulate the journey over the Oregon Trail from the planning stages through arrival at their destination. Excellent graphics, good instructions and plenty of options to explore allow students to create their own experiences of the fun and challenges of travel through the wilderness.

★ *Pecos Bill.* Rabbit Ears Productions, 1988 (videocassette, 30 minutes). 4–8. Robin Williams narrates this delightful, knee-slapping rendition of the famous tall tales as Pecos Bill invents the cattle drive, rides his trusty cougar mount, cracks his rattlesnake whip and carves out the Grand Canyon riding a wild tornado.

★ *The Song of Sacajawea* by James Howard Kunstler. Rabbit Ears Productions, 1992 (videocassette, 30 minutes). 4–8. Laura Dern narrates this American Heroes & Legends series title. Breathtaking illustrations support the moving story, which not only celebrates the life of Sacajawea, but also effectively summarizes the goals, experiences and accomplishments of the Lewis and Clark Expedition.

Web sites

★ *The Cherokee Trail of Tears*
rosecity.net/tears

★ *The Underground Railroad*
www.nationalgeographic.com/features/99/railroad

★ *West Across America with Lewis and Clark*
www.nationalgeographic.com/features/97/west

★ *The Wild West*
www.thewildwest.org

Activities on Westward Expansion and Frontier Life

★ Discussion Prompts

Use these prompts to stimulate discussion of themes and issues of the frontier period.

★ **Manifest Destiny.** In *Daily Life in a Covered Wagon*, the author mentions that the Manifest Destiny of the United States was to control all the land from the Atlantic to the Pacific. The phrase was first used by a newspaper editor named John Louis O'Sullivan in 1845 to express a growing attitude among Americans, and it quickly caught on. It meant that because American ideas of freedom, civilization and government were so wonderful, the new nation had the right to claim all the land that now makes up the continental United States and to impose its way of life on everyone in it. The government used this lofty expression to justify taking land from Native Americans and from Mexican rancheros in the Southwest, and to inspire people to settle all across the continent. Using these questions and all you have learned about this period, discuss the concept and its results.

- Who did the idea of Manifest Destiny help? Who did it hurt?

- Does the attitude of confidence and idealism it implies describe the early explorers and settlers of the new nation? Does it still describe Americans today?

- How did the concept affect characters in stories from this chapter's bibliography? You might talk about members of Lewis and Clark's Corps of Discovery (this was before the phrase was used, but not before the idea of the American right to control the land was prevalent); Francis Tucket in *Mr. Tucket*; Bright Moon in *Sing Down the Moon;* or Annie, Righteous and Charity in *Remember My Name.*

- Was the idea of Manifest Destiny justified? Why or why not?

★ **A Diverse Cast of Characters.** People from many countries and cultures helped build the nation during this exciting period. There were explorers, traders and trappers, mountain men, trailblazers, farmers, cowboys, gold-diggers, lawmen and outlaws, orphans, teachers, ped- dlers, preachers and missionaries, immigrant laborers, Native American guides, advocates for Native rights and many more. Invite students to choose a favorite character from one of the books and discuss how each character contributed to the process of settling the country and making it what it is today. Interesting characters to discuss might be Mr. Grimes from *Mr. Tucket;* James Weaver from *Soon Be Free;* Polly and Jessie from *Bluestem;* Otter in *Dragon's Gate;* the woman in *I Have Heard of a Land;* Sacajawea; or Chief Seattle from *Brother Eagle, Sister Sky.* To add a light-hearted twist to the discussion, you might include *Swamp Angel* or *Pecos Bill.*

★ **Why Be a Pioneer?** In *Mississippi Mud, Daily Life in a Covered Wagon, I Have Heard of a Land, Bluestem, The Journey Home* and *The Borning Room,* we read about the huge dangers and hardships of traveling west to settle the frontier and of living in the primitive conditions of the period. Discuss with the class why settlers chose to brave the hardships on the frontier, using these prompts. Use examples of characters from the stories to illustrate your ideas.

- What were the settlers seeking? What motivated them to make the journey and take the risks? What did they hope to gain?

- What were the greatest struggles and sorrows of the pioneers? What were their greatest pleasures and joys?

- Did they find what they were seeking in the West?

- What qualities do you think were most important to success on the frontier?

- Based on what you know about the experiences of the pioneers, would you have chosen to leave civilization behind and make a new life on the frontier? Why or why not?

★ Games

★ **Crossword Puzzle.** Enjoy the crossword puzzle found on the reproducible handout on page 38, based on terms and phrases used during this period.

- ★ **Board games** were popular pastimes for pioneer children and families. Chess, checkers and backgammon were common. Some board games were designed to teach children religious and moral lessons. A version of Chutes and Ladders had children advancing on ladders to heaven for doing good deeds and losing ground to snakes, symbolic of the Biblical story of the fall from grace in the Garden of Eden, for misbehaving. Take some time to enjoy these games we still play today.

- ★ **"Load the Wagons!"** Surviving the trip overland to your new home on the frontier depended partly on careful preparation. Make a game of planning what to take on the journey. Divide the class into teams. About six students per team works well and approximates the size of a family. Using tape to mark dimensions on the floor and wall of a corner of the classroom or hallway, show the size of a typical covered wagon used by pioneers— about 12' long, 4' wide, with solid sides about 3' high. The fabric cover might add sheltered space for a total of 6' tall at the highest point. Have students review pages 8–11 of *Daily Life in a Covered Wagon*. Each team should carefully plan what they'll need for their trip. Their task is to create a list of everything they will pack into the wagon and a plan for packing it. The challenge is that everything must fit into the space allowed, with trail supplies accessible! Keep in mind that too little food or supplies will leave you starving and needy on the trail, or ill equipped to set up your claim. But too much may be too heavy for your oxen to pull up the steep mountain trails and have to be discarded along the way. Remind students to consider the seasons of travel (spring through fall) and the cool temperatures in the mountains. Encourage them to use the measured space and available boxes or objects in the classroom to test out their plan. Once each team has completed its list and its plan for packing, have teams explain their lists and plans to the class. After the presentations, have students vote on which wagonload they would choose to depend upon for their journey overland! Give the winning team a small prize.

★ Artistic/Creative Expressions

- ★ **Tellers of Tall Tales.** Watch *Pecos Bill* and read *Swamp Angel* with the class. Talk about the genre of tall tales and invite students to write and illustrate their own tall tales of humorous, superhuman achievements or a tall tale explaining the origins of natural landmarks or phenomena.

- ★ **Westward Expansion Puzzles.** Have students create a picture illustrating a scene in one of the books for this chapter. Make the drawings into jigsaw puzzles by backing them with card stock or cardboard and cutting them into appropriately sized pieces for the class. (You can make a master pattern for cutting the puzzles or buy one at a craft or educational materials supply store.) Keep each puzzle in its own folder, so the pieces don't get mixed up. Return the puzzles to the artists and pair students up. Each pair of students will swap puzzles, put them together and try to guess what event from the period or what scene from which book is depicted.

- ★ **Tin Punch Craft.** Pioneers used lots of creativity and minimal materials and resources to make their homes more pleasant. Tin was inexpensive, lightweight and versatile for many uses. You will need:

  paper
  a pencil
  tape
  an aluminum foil pie plate
  heavy cardboard
  a nail and hammer

- • Draw a simple design on the paper with the pencil. Here are some ideas to get you started.

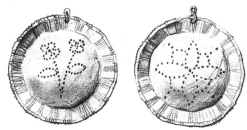

- • Tape the paper to the pie plate.

- • Place the cardboard on the tabletop to protect the surface as you hammer. Gently hammer in the nail at even intervals along the outline of the design.

- To hang, punch a hole in the top of the rim.

- To make a candle shield, cut straight across the bottom of the pie plate and bend the plate into a curve. Stand this up in front of a lit candle in a candleholder. Pioneers often used shields (called *sconces*) to keep the candle from blowing out or to protect the wall from the smoke and heat.

★ **A Family to Follow.** Continue the activity from the first two chapters through this and later periods of American history studied.

★ Practical Crafts

★ **Candlemaking.** Making candles was a regular chore for settlers, who relied on them for light. Everyday candles were made of sheep or beef tallow, but for special occasions, beeswax or bayberry wax was used. Follow these steps to make simple beeswax candles.

- Buy candlewick and sheets of honeycomb at a craft store.

- Use a knife to cut the wax into strips as wide as you want the candles to be tall, and cut the wick into sections about ½" longer than the width of the wax strips.

- Cover a craft table with soft cloth. A towel works well.

- Spread out the wax strips on the cloth-covered table. Lay the wicks across the near ends of the wax strips, extending ½" beyond one end. Roll the wax gently and firmly around the wick, the whole length of the strip, to create the candle.

★ **International Pioneer Pancakes.** Pioneers often made pancakes because they were cheap, filling and tasty. As pioneers reached the West from different parts of the world, they brought along varieties of pancakes as part of their traditional cuisine. Experiment with ethnic variations of the basic pancake, keeping in mind the settlers who enjoyed them and shared them with their neighbors! Arrange to use a home economics room or school kitchen. You might enlist a home economics teacher to help with this activity. Divide the class into four groups and have each group work on one of the variations. Cut the results into bite-sized bits and share. If you're really ambitious, you might use a standard waffle recipe and have one group make waffles, as Dutch settlers did, and serve them with butter and syrup or honey.

Ingredients for basic pancake recipe:

1 cup flour

1 teaspoon baking powder

½ teaspoon salt

1½ tablespoons sugar

1 egg

¾ cup milk

3 tablespoons oil or melted butter

- Mix dry ingredients in a large bowl. Beat egg and add milk and oil or butter in a smaller bowl. Blend wet ingredients into dry ingredients. Because conditions vary, you may need to add a little milk or flour to get the consistency you want. Heat a little oil on a medium-hot griddle and pour in just enough batter to make a four- to five-inch pancake. When the edges begin to brown and bubbles appear on top, flip the pancake and brown the other side. Cakes can be kept warm in a 200° oven.

- Group one will make the basic recipe of pioneer flapjacks. They should be served with butter and maple syrup, honey or molasses.

- Group two will add a little more milk, to make a pancake thinner than the flapjack. These were called blinis by Russian settlers or blintzes by Jewish settlers. They were served folded over a mixture of cottage cheese and sugar, and topped with a fruit sauce.

- Group three will add even more milk to the basic recipe to make a fairly runny batter that will cook into thin pancakes, called crepes by French pioneers. They should be rolled around bits of fresh fruit and served with cream.

- Group four will make the basic recipe and serve it as Swedish pioneers did, with berry jam and powdered sugar on top.

Research Projects

Invite students to try these opportunities to explore westward expansion and frontier life as individual or small group projects, or involve the whole class.

★ **A Growing Nation!** Two major processes contributed to the nation's growth during the period from the Declaration of Independence to the twentieth century. One was the acquisition of land, and the other the organization of territories and, finally, states in those newly acquired lands. Have one group of students research land acquisition (e.g., the Louisiana Purchase, the Texas Annexation). Another group can track the gradual organization of the continental United States into territories and states. Students should create maps and timelines, as appropriate, to share their findings. Basic reference books in the school media center will provide this information.

★ **Environmental Impact.** One consequence of the rapid settlement of the West was great changes to natural ecosystems. Papa in *Night of the Full Moon* expresses concern about these changes. Forests were clear-cut to make farm fields; many species of animals were hunted to near-extinction. Buffalo all but disappeared from the plains. Beavers were overtrapped to meet the European demand for felt. Passenger pigeons, pests who damaged crops, were killed off entirely. Invite students to research what happened to these and other animal species, and report their findings to the class. Use the Internet to research the period and its impact on individual species.

★ **Daniel Boone and Life on the Frontier.** Reread *Daniel Boone*. The poem offers an excellent opportunity to bring the history of the frontier alive for students. Boone became a "bigger than life" symbol of the frontier spirit, and the many indirect references to historical events in the poem can be approached as a puzzle for the class to solve. Follow the steps below. The reproducible worksheet and teacher's resource on pages 36–37 will help direct student efforts. This is a complex activity, and might be most appropriate for grades 6–8.

• As a class, create a timeline of events alluded to in the poem. Use the order and the words of the poem ("French and Indian War," "Wilderness Road," "Down the fort in a wave of flame...," etc.).

• Assign a group of students to research each event. Help them, as needed, to identify the event clearly for further research.

• Have each group fill in the timeline with the correct date and identifying information (1775—Wilderness Road opened, 1776—Revolutionary War, 1778—Boonesborough Siege, etc.).

• Have each group create and present a poem, song, skit or poster that shares what they've learned about their event.

Students may want to learn more about Daniel Boone. Refer them to the school media center and the Internet. There are several interesting Web sites on the famous frontiersman.

Daniel Boone Research Project

Complete this worksheet to help you organize your research and work with your group.

My group's reference from the poem is: _____

The reference in the poem is about this event: _____

This event happened in what year? _____

I used these sources to learn about this event: _____

_____

_____

Here's what I learned about this historical event (continue on the back if needed):

_____

_____

_____

_____

_____

_____

_____

_____

_____

_____

My group is creating a: **POEM**   **SKIT**   **SONG**   **POSTER**   to express what we learned.
(Circle one)

Daniel Boone Research Project
Teacher's Resource—Timeline of Events

These references from Guiterman's poem make up the timeline of events. To save time as you set up this project, you'll find: the reference; its location in the poem by stanza and line; and the event referred to.

1. **"Home from the French and Indian War"** (First stanza, line 3): Boone served under British General Braddock in 1755, as they marched to try to take Fort Duquesne.

2. **"He married his maid with a golden band"** (First stanza, line 5): In 1755, Boone married Rebecca Bryan. Have this group research Boone's marriage and family life. What kind of family man was Boone? How did Rebecca manage with her husband gone so much?

3. **"'Elbow room!' laughed Daniel Boone"** (First stanza, last line): This refers to one of several times when Boone felt the territory was getting too crowded and moved farther into the wilderness. Students can track these moves of Boone and his family and talk about the wanderlust and solitary nature of many early explorers and pioneers.

4. **"On the Wilderness Road that his axemen made"** (Second stanza, line 1): In 1775, Boone headed a group of woodsmen to open a trail connecting existing Indian trails to Kentucky for the Transylvania Company. They created the famous Wilderness Road, traveled by many pioneers in the following years.

5. **"When the land said 'Nay!' to the stubborn king"** (Second stanza, line 6): An obvious reference to the Declaration of Independence and Revolutionary War. There are contradictory reports of Boone's involvement in the war. He probably did his part to protect the new nation by "guarding its west-ward gate" from Indian attacks. This group might look at how the Revolutionary War affected early settlers on the frontier.

6. **"Daniel Boone from a surge of hate / Guarded a nation's westward gate"** (Second stanza, lines 9–10): This reference and the next few lines refer to the Boonesborough Siege of 1778.

7. **"He launched his bateau on Ohio's breast"** (Third stanza, line 3): At age 65, Boone was again attacked by wanderlust and traveled the Ohio River to settle on a land grant near St. Louis, Missouri. His time there makes for very interesting reading.

8. **"So he turned his face where the stars are strewn"** (Third stanza, line 19): This is a reference to Boone's death in 1819. Have this group look at the fanciful depiction of Boone in the next world, sorting out the images and symbols and finding parallels to activities and events in Boone's life (e.g., paddling his canoe down the Milky Way evokes his river travels). They might consider Boone's role in American cultural tradition as a legendary hero.

Westward Expansion Crossword Puzzle

Complete the crossword puzzle, using terms and phrases from your reading about this period in American history.

Across

1. ___ trains carried needy children to new homes in the West.

6. The ___ Act offered free land to settlers.

8. The ___ Railroad moved runaway slaves to freedom in the North.

9. A tall ___ is a bigger-than-life story about a famous character.

Down

2. enjoying the lunch break during a wagon train

3. beginner, used to describe new immigrants

4. prairie settlers' home made of sod

5. bread made of cornmeal

7. popular musical instrument during pioneer times

Answers Across: 1. Orphan; 6. Homestead; 8. Underground; 9. tale **Down:** 2. nooning; 3. greenhorn; 4. soddie; 5. johnnycake; 7. fiddle

The Civil War and Reconstruction

The issues and conflicts dividing our young nation, South from North, had been building for decades when Lincoln became President in 1861. Even when those hoping to avoid war had to abandon that hope, both sides expected a short and decisive confrontation. Instead, the next four years produced the world's first "modern war," complete with unprecedented carnage, incomprehensible losses, fearsome new weapons and military strategies and profound divisions of conviction and attitude not yet healed today.

There were many different realities for those fighting the battles. Leaders and generals on both sides pondered compelling issues and details of military strategy while young soldiers on both sides proclaimed grand ideals, entertained dreams of glory and struggled with fear. Even within their own ranks, there was confusion and disagreement about the causes of war. Was the real issue slavery or states' rights? The honor of the South or preservation of the Union? The increasingly different economies and lifestyles of the North and South? Control of the western frontier?

For all concerned, the terrible hardships of hunger, cold, disease, boredom and the horrors of battle brought discouragement and disillusionment. Images of the Civil War, including devastation and heroism, brutality and simple human dignity, still haunt the nation's consciousness.

Some themes of this period to explore through literature include:

★ The causes of the war: What were we fighting for?

★ Major conflicts and battles.

★ The face of "modern warfare."

★ The costs of war.

★ Heroes, leaders and famous figures.

★ Healing the divided nation.

Some additional series that might enrich your exploration include:

★ The Civil War titles from The American War Library. Lucent Books. 6–8.

★ Untold History of the Civil War. Chelsea House Publishers. 5–8.

★ Young Readers' History of the Civil War. Lodestar Books. 5–8.

Resources on the Civil War and Reconstruction

⭐ Fiction

★ *Across Five Aprils* by Irene Hunt. Berkley Publishing Group, 2002. 5–8. Newbery Honor Book. As much a commentary on the progress of the war as a story of its impact on the fictional Creighton family, this title brings the period alive. We see through the eyes of young Jethro, who must deal with fear and loss, illness and death, the defection of his favorite brother to the Rebel cause, and the need to shoulder a man's responsibilities before his time. Very rich historical and character drama.

★ *Be Ever Hopeful, Hannalee* by Patricia Beatty. Troll, 1990. 5–8. Surviving members of Hannalee's Georgia family move to Atlanta to seek a better future after the war. Reconstruction Atlanta is living under martial law, humming with activity and seeking workers to rebuild the city. Spunky Hannalee helps her family find work, frees her older brother from wrongful arrest and makes some unlikely friends. Readers learn much about the tensions and challenges of the period and find much to hope for in Hannalee's friendships with a Yankee girl and a newly freed slave.

★ *The Blue and the Gray* by Eve Bunting. Scholastic, 2001. 4–6. Two young friends look forward to being neighbors when they move into their new houses being built near an open field. The boys, one white and one black, learn about the Civil War battle that raged in that unmarked field. They vow to remember and honor those who fought and died for their beliefs. A touching, healing message.

★ *Bonds of Affection* by Graham DuBois. *Plays: The Drama Magazine for Young People*, January/February 1999, pages 11–17. 4–8. When the Hansom family is caught in Gettysburg looking for the son who has been missing since the battle, old family friend Abraham Lincoln pays them a visit and intervenes for them with Union troops. Portrayed with compassion, humility and wit, Lincoln wins over even Robert, the son and Confederate soldier.

★ *Drummer Boy: Marching to the Civil War* by Ann Turner. HarperCollins, 1999. 4–6. A 13-year-old farm boy hears President Lincoln speak, lies about his age and joins the Union army. As a drummer boy, he helps wake the soldiers, cheer and hearten them and carry orders to them in battle through drum rhythms. He reports seeing things that "no boy should see." Lush illustrations draw the reader into the boy's haunting experiences.

★ *Here and Then* by George Ella Lyon. Troll, 1997. 4–7. Abby joins her parents on a Civil War reenactment weekend, where she gets more than she bargained for. The character she's playing, a nurse famous for her compassion for wounded Union and Confederate soldiers alike, draws Abby back in time and into her desperate search for medical supplies. Abby and her best friend face an adventure and end up with a puzzle as satisfying as it is unexplainable. Strong, credible characters make this gripping story work.

★ *Jayhawker* by Patricia Beatty. Morrow Junior Books, 1995. 6–8. Lije Tully, 12-year-old Kansas farm boy, joins his father's activities as a Jayhawker—an anti-slavery raider. When he sees his father killed on a raid, Lije vows revenge. He becomes a spy among the enemy Missouri Bushwhackers, and sees the worst of battle and violence. Along the way he encounters such notable characters as John Brown, William Quantrill, Jesse James and Wild Bill Hickok. In typical style, award-winning historical novelist Beatty gives us lots of action and plenty to think about.

★ *Moon Over Tennessee: A Boy's Civil War Journal* by Craig Crist-Evans. Houghton Mifflin, 1999. 4–8. A 13-year-old Tennessee farm boy accompanies his father to help around camp while his father serves as a Confederate soldier. This fictional journal, written in eloquent prose poem style, shares his intensely personal experience of the details and costs of war. Evocative black-and-white wood engravings complement the deceptively simple, straightforward text.

★ *Pink and Say* by Patricia Polacco. Philomel Books, 1994. 4–6. Polacco tells the true story of her great-great-grandfather's experience in the Civil War, when he was left for dead on a Georgia battlefield at age 15. The book is a tribute to the young African American soldier who found him and took him to safety in his home, where his mother helped both boys recover. The painfully touching story with its sad ending dramatically personalizes aspects of the war not often discussed.

★ *Rifles for Watie* by Harold Keith. Econo-Clad, 1989. 6–8. Newbery Medal Book. This 1957 classic, occasionally flawed by stereotypes and caricature, is perhaps the most wide-ranging Civil War novel for young people. Its ambitious scope works because of well-developed characters (like the protagonist, Jefferson Davis Bussey) who defy stereotypes and win readers' interest and sympathy. At age 16, Jeff joins Kansas volunteers to fight for the Union, full of naïve dreams of glory. Over the course of the war we experience with Jeff the roles of infantryman, artillery soldier, cavalryman and scout, as well as spy with Rebel forces. Set in the Western Theater of the war, the book exposes us to Bushwhackers and Native Americans and explores the different issues and causes at stake for them. We learn about weapons, medical care, military propaganda, informal truces between opposing front-line soldiers and the very cruel realities of war. Throw in lots of battle action and a little romance, and you have a first-rate story.

★ *Run the Blockade* by G. Clifton Wisler. HarperCollins, 2000. 6–8. This book looks at how our Civil War affected those outside the U.S. Fourteen-year-old Henry goes to sea on a British ship running the Union's blockade of southern seaports to bring out cotton, without which England's clothing factories are stalled and its workers impoverished. Henry is a winning character with the sea in his blood, a taste for adventure and a sincere desire to provide for his poor family in Ireland. Lots of action and an unusual viewpoint.

★ *Silent Thunder: A Civil War Story* by Andrea Davis Pinkney. Hyperion Books for Children, 2001. 5–7. Roscoe and Summer, slave children in Virginia, take turns telling about their lives and dreams in 1862. Summer hungers to learn to read, while her older brother is determined to win freedom fighting for the Union. An "up-close and personal" look at life as a plantation slave.

★ *Sweet Clara and the Freedom Quilt* by Deborah Hopkinson. Alfred A. Knopf, 1995. 4–8. Young Clara is a slave, taken from her mother to labor on another plantation. She learns to sew, goes into the Big House as a seamstress and creates a quilt that serves as a secret map to connect runaways with the Underground Railroad. Based on a true story, this picture book tells of Clara's trip to freedom and of others who followed her quilt map.

★ *With Every Drop of Blood: A Novel of the Civil War* by James Lincoln Collier and Christopher Collier. Econo-Clad, 1999. 7–8. Eager for revenge and adventure, 14-year-old Johnny forgets his promise to his Rebel father, who died of battle wounds, and runs off to help carry supplies to Rebel troops. A black Union soldier captures him. In spite of themselves, the two become friends and ultimately risk their lives to save each other. As they endure the final days of the war on the run, they ponder the causes and issues of the war and the future ahead of them.

★ Nonfiction

★ *The Civil War for Kids: A History with 21 Activities* by Janis Herbert. Chicago Review Press, 1999. 4–8. Lively text, expressive black-and-white illustrations and a good resource section at the end support the emphasis on activities in this inviting introduction. There are many brief biographical sketches and interesting definitions of terms and expressions used during the war.

★ *Civil War: A Library of Congress Book* by Martin W. Sandler. HarperCollins, 2000. 4–8. This visually appealing picture book overview of the causes, course and aftermath of the war is an accessible source of basic information and a start-off point for further research. Concise, heavily illustrated spreads tell the story in bite-sized chunks. The present-tense narration is both compelling and distracting.

★ *The Gettysburg Address* by Abraham Lincoln. Houghton Mifflin, 1998. 4–8. This dramatic picture book presentation of Lincoln's eloquent 272 words of dedication begs to be read aloud with appropriate background music. An interesting forward and splendid, somber, black-and-white illustrations set the brief remarks in context and make them seem even more extraordinary.

★ *Lincoln: A Photobiography* by Russell Freedman. Houghton Mifflin, 1989. 5–8. Newbery Medal Book. In this warm, lively and honest biography, Lincoln's weaknesses are set forth along with his strengths, and the opinions of his detractors alongside those of his supporters. A probing and readable account of this most beloved of America's presidents.

★ ***Reconstruction and Reform*** by Joy Hakim. Oxford University Press, 1994. 5–8. This A History of U.S. series title both offers an overview of post-war reconstruction in the South and ties together the contents of the past, current and next chapters of this book. In a lively style and appealing format with short chapters and lots of illustrations and sidebars, Hakim explores issues, events, movements and influential people of the period, broadening our narrowed Civil War focus back out to the diverse activities and concerns of a continent-wide nation.

⭐ Other Media

★ ***The Red Badge of Courage*** by Stephen Crane. Warner Brothers Classics, 2001 (videocassette). 5–8. This reissue of the 1951 black-and-white classic holds up quite well, with some breaches of twenty-first century sensibilities. Farm boy-turned-soldier Henry shares his powerfully personal experiences of the chaos and confusion, the drudgery and drama of the War Between the States, and his timeless struggle with cowardice and courage in battle. Crane's brilliant sensory imagery is translated into some stunning visual moments in film.

★ ***Songs of the Civil War.*** New World Records, 1992 (CD). 4–8. This celebrity collection of Civil War tunes features Kathy Mattea, Richie Havens, Waylon Jennings and other performers who may be familiar to students. The old marching standards are here, along with some of the melancholy ballads of the period.

★ ***Voices of Valor: Words of the Civil War*** narrated by Frank E. VanDiver. Texas A & M University Press, 1994 (audiocassette). 4–8. VanDiver shares causes and key moments of the Civil War through famous speeches, song lyrics and personal letters of the period, accompanied by Civil War music. Stirring words, set in context through effective commentary, provide an interesting look at both everyday and extraordinary emotions of this dramatic time.

⭐ Web sites

★ ***The American Civil War*** americancivilwar.com

★ ***American Memory Library of Congress Selected Civil War Photographs*** memory.loc.gov/ammem/cwphtml/ cwphome.html

★ ***Civil War in Miniature*** www.civilwarmini.com

★ ***The CWi Civil War Cookbook*** www.civilwarinteractive.com/cookbook.htm

Activities on the Civil War and Reconstruction

Discussion Prompts

Use these prompts to generate discussion of themes and issues of the Civil War.

★ **Causes of the Civil War.** Many books on the list, including *The Civil War: A Library of Congress Book*, *Drummer Boy*, *Pink and Say*, *The Secret to Freedom*, *Jayhawker*, *Rifles for Watie*, *Be Ever Hopeful, Hannalee* and *With Every Drop of Blood*, talk about the causes of the Civil War.

- What were the major issues that led to war?

- What might a Union soldier answer if you asked what he was fighting for?

- What might a Confederate soldier answer to the same question? Would all Rebel soldiers give the same answer?

- How about an African American?

- Why did Native Americans join the fight? For whom did they fight, and why?

- Do the characters in the books in this chapter, on both sides of the conflict, believe they are fighting for the right cause? Support your answer with examples from the stories.

★ **Advantages and Disadvantages of the North and South.** Discuss the advantages and disadvantages of each side in the War Between the States. Talk about how they changed during the course of the war. You might make a chart on large paper to keep track of the ideas. Consider clarity of purpose, population, resources, agricultural vs. industrial economies, morale over time and the location of the fighting. Use examples from the books to illustrate how people felt the impact of these advantages and disadvantages throughout the war. (For example, characters in *Jayhawkers* talked about fighting to protect their own homes, families and communities. Still, the fighting in the South depleted its resources and morale until the Confederate army had to surrender.)

★ **Reconstruction.** In *Lincoln: A Photobiography* we read of Lincoln's hope, near the end of the war, that the whole nation would act, "With malice toward none; with charity for all … to bind up the nation's wounds…." Lincoln didn't live to oversee Reconstruction. Referring to *Reconstruction and Reform, Be Ever Hopeful, Hannalee* and other resources, discuss the nation's efforts and challenges in trying to recover from the Civil War.

- What steps did the U.S. government take to rebuild southern cities and the economy of the South?

- How did the government try to help newly freed African Americans? How did southern whites feel about these measures?

- How were conditions better for African Americans after the war? What danger and challenges did freedom bring former slaves?

- Had you lived during the Reconstruction period, what suggestions would you have given the President and Congress, or your fellow citizens, to help bring the country together and make it strong?

Games

★ **Wordsearch.** Try the wordsearch found on the reproducible on page 47, based on terms and phrases used during this period. For younger grades, you might challenge students to see how many of the words they can find, rather than expecting them to find all of the words.

★ **Send a "Wigwag" Message.** Civil War ships used a system of flag signals, called "Wigwag," to send messages between ships. To play, you will need:

  4 people
  a flag or an old towel attached to a stick
  paper
  pencil

- Have two players send the signals and the other two receive them. The pair reading the message should write down the signal numbers and later decode them into letters.

- Only five different signals will be used to represent the 26 letters of the alphabet. Use the chart on page 44 to determine which signals you should use for each letter of your message.

  Starting position (also used between letters): Hold the flagstaff with one hand at the bottom and the other in the middle.

Hold the flag above your head in an upright position. Pause at the starting position for three seconds between letters.

Signal 1: From the starting position, wave the flag to your right, stopping at your waist, then bring it back up to the starting position.

Starting Position   Signal 1

Signal 2: From the starting position, wave the flag to your right, all the way to the ground, then return to the starting position.

Signal 3: From the starting position, wave the flag to your left, stopping at your waist, then bring it back up to the starting position.

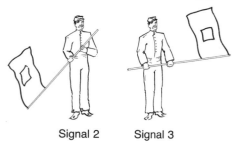

Signal 2   Signal 3

Signal 4: From the starting position, wave the flag to your left, all the way to the ground, then return to the starting position.

Signal 5: From the starting position, lower the flag in front of you all the way to the ground, then return to the starting position.

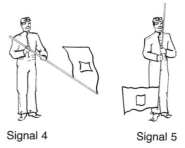

Signal 4   Signal 5

- A sample message, "Aim Right," would require these signals:

A   Signal 1
I   Signal 5 + Signal 4
M   Signal 5 twice + Signal 3

R   Signal 5 three times + Signal 3
I   Signal 5 + Signal 4
G   Signal 5 + Signal 2
H   Signal 5 + Signal 3
T   Signal 5 four times

Alphabet Chart	
A	Signal 1
B	Signal 2
C	Signal 3
D	Signal 4
E	Signal 5
F	Signal 5 quickly followed by Signal 1
G	Signal 5 + Signal 2
H	Signal 5 + Signal 3
I	Signal 5 + Signal 4
J	Signal 5 twice
K	Signal 5 twice + Signal 1
L	Signal 5 twice + Signal 2
M	Signal 5 twice + Signal 3
N	Signal 5 twice + Signal 4
O	Signal 5 three times
P	Signal 5 three times + Signal 1
Q	Signal 5 three times + Signal 2
R	Signal 5 three times + Signal 3
S	Signal 5 three times + Signal 4
T	Signal 5 four times
U	Signal 5 four times + Signal 1
V	Signal 5 four times + Signal 2
W	Signal 5 four times + Signal 3
X	Signal 5 four times + Signal 4
Y	Signal 5 five times + Signal 1
Z	Signal 5 five times + Signal 2

★ **Civil War Trivia.** Students will create this game as they study the Civil War, and play it at the end of the unit for fun and review.

- As you begin the unit, assign each student to write at least one multiple-choice question about a detail of the period that interests him or her during the reading and study. Students should write questions on index cards, complete with answer options and the correct answer circled. Encourage them to find questions that are challenging but answerable from resources at hand. For example, "Who was the head of the Confederate Army?" is too easy. A good sample question might be, "Who was Grace Bedell?" (Answer: She was a child who wrote to Abraham Lincoln, suggesting that he grow a beard to help him win the presidential election in 1860. See pages 61–62 in *Lincoln: A Photobiography* or page 6 in *The Civil War for Kids*.)

- At the end of the unit, see that each student has submitted at least one question. Review and edit them as needed.

- Divide the class into teams of six or fewer to play the game. Have them sit in groups, assign each team a color and give them a sign in that color to help you keep track. You will be both moderator and scorekeeper.

- Shuffle the question cards and deal out "hands," making sure that each team has the same number of questions to answer. This will equalize the chances of a team getting questions written by its own members. Don't distribute the hands to the teams. Keep them with you, marked with a colored marker to indicate which stack belongs to which team.

- Drawing a card from the appropriate stack, ask the first team their first question out loud. They may consult to come up with an answer. If the team answers the question correctly without using resources beyond their own knowledge, they get two points. If not, have the team write down the question for research in the second round of the game.

- Follow the same procedure for each team, rotating through the teams and questions until all questions are either answered or assigned for research.

- At the end of round one, review team scores. Then give the teams a limited amount of time (perhaps 15 minutes) to use classroom or media center resources to find the answers to their remaining questions. Teams should cooperate to answer as many questions correctly as possible.

- At the end of the research time, reconvene the class in teams and give them turns reading questions with their best answers until all questions have been addressed. A correct answer in round two is worth one point.

- Tally the final scores (round one score plus round two score), and announce the winning team, awarding a small prize or privilege as appropriate.

Note: If you want to make the game more subjective, you might invite students to embellish the story by telling more about the subject addressed in the question. Good additional information could earn an extra point.

★ Artistic/Creative Expressions

★ **Play Time!** Prepare and present the play, *Bonds of Affection*. If your school does not subscribe to *Plays* magazine, contact the publication for permission. You might invite another class to watch the performance, or offer it as an assembly program for the school.

★ **Famous Civil War Quotations.** The Civil War produced many memorable speeches and famous quotations that are still remembered and used today. Introduce this activity by playing excerpts from the *Voices of Valor* audiocassette. Then assign each student to use books from the bibliography and other classroom resources to find a brief quotation from the period that is still meaningful today. (For example, General Sherman's often-quoted, "War is hell," or Admiral Farragut's, "Damn the torpedoes! Full speed ahead!") Students will make illustrated posters of their chosen quotes to post around the classroom. They should explain why they chose their particular quotation.

★ **Lee's Surrender.** Few scenes from the Civil War are as moving or as full of respect and compassion as Lee's surrender to Grant at Appomattox. Review accounts of the meeting between the two Generals on pages 129–130 of *The Civil War for Kids* and page 78 of *Civil War: A Library of Congress Book*. Then either listen to Lee's farewell speech to his troops on the *Voices of Valor* audiocassette, or stage a dramatic reading of the speech by an expressive reader in the class, accompanied by appropriate background music.

★ **Creative Response.** Have students create poems, songs or journal entries reflecting the Civil War experience of their favorite characters from their reading.

⭐ Practical Crafts

★ **Message Quilts.** Review *Sweet Clara and the Freedom Quilt* and the information on page 12 of *The Civil War for Kids*. These books tell how anti-slavery activists used quilt patterns to send messages to slaves wanting to escape to freedom, either by assigning secret meanings to traditional patterns or by designing hidden messages or maps directing slaves along the Underground Railroad into quilt patterns. Have teams of students put themselves in the role of Clara and try their hand at designing a coded message or map into a small paper quilt. Teams should share their designs and explain their intended meanings.

★ **Hoppin' John.** Try this recipe from the Confederate South. You'll need access to a good kitchen. One recipe serves eight.

Ingredients:

> 5 slices bacon
>
> 2 medium onions
>
> 2 medium green peppers
>
> 2 cups white rice
>
> 1 can cooked black-eyed peas
>
> salt and pepper

- Fry bacon until crisp. Blot cooked bacon on paper towels to absorb grease, and crumble into bits. Coarsely chop onions and peppers, and brown them in the pan with the bacon grease. Cook rice according to package directions, adding the browned onion and green pepper as the rice boils. When rice is tender and water absorbed, add drained black-eyed peas, bacon bits and salt and pepper to taste, then heat to serve.

⭐ Research Projects

Invite students to use these opportunities to explore the Civil War period as individual or small group projects, or involve the whole class.

★ **"The First Modern War."** The American Civil War is referred to as the first modern war because of many new weapons and forms of military strategy used in it. Invite interested students to research some of the new inventions and "firsts" of the war. Students should report their findings to the class, with appropriate visual aids. Some firsts to consider might include the following:

- Repeater rifles (These play an important role in *Rifles for Watie*.)

- Ironclad warships (These are discussed in *Run the Blockade*.)

- Lightweight artillery

- Trench warfare

- Aerial spy balloons

- Medal of Honor (Awarded to the main character in *Rifles for Watie*.)

The chapter entitled, "A Modern War" in *Civil War: A Library of Congress Book* is a good starting point for this activity.

★ **War by the Numbers.** The Civil War was a war of impressive, and sometimes tragic, numbers. Use the reproducible handout on page 49 to explore noteworthy statistics of the war.

★ **Visiting or Visitor.** Have the class look into whether there is a Civil War museum, battlefield, cemetery or reenactment group nearby. The American Civil War Web site, http://www.sunsite.utk.edu/civil-war/warweb.html, is a good source of information for locating these sites or groups. Follow up with a field trip to a nearby site. Or invite a member of a Civil War reenactment group to visit the class and share his or her experiences.

★ **Adopt-A-Veteran.** Some veterans' organizations or reenactment groups sponsor "adopt-a-vet" programs to help people learn more about the war. The American Civil War Web site mentioned above will direct you to at least one of these groups, to see what's involved. If there isn't a group near you that offers such a program, consider choosing a Civil War veteran from your area, or maybe veterans from both the Union and Confederate armies, and learning about him or them as suggested by "adopt-a-vet" programs.

Civil War Word Search

Review the bolded words and their definitions on page 48. Then find and circle the words on the grid below. They may read up, down, across, diagonally or backwards.

```
L  G  B  S  C  C  C  Q  F  W  B  T  A  E  R
N  O  K  O  O  A  T  U  D  E  U  S  N  H  P
C  Z  S  V  N  V  A  K  K  D  S  I  T  D  P
A  D  U  E  F  A  N  L  L  A  H  N  I  P  U
H  X  Q  R  E  L  T  H  S  K  W  O  E  L  C
Z  X  X  E  D  R  V  S  P  C  H  I  T  E  U
K  O  Z  I  E  Y  I  X  T  O  A  T  A  T  N
Y  T  B  G  R  N  S  E  E  L  C  I  M  G  N
F  T  Z  N  A  W  N  E  S  B  K  L  Z  J  X
D  A  C  T  C  O  K  L  N  D  E  O  R  I  T
L  M  I  Y  Y  N  A  G  T  T  R  B  U  P  I
U  O  C  A  A  V  R  R  E  P  E  A  T  E  R
N  P  B  Y  E  E  V  N  J  P  Z  R  F  K  L
B  P  K  R  S  V  W  I  T  A  H  P  Y  T  J
J  A  Y  H  A  W  K  E  R  U  S  W  V  B  S
```

abolitionist

Antietam

Appomattox

assassination

bayonet

blockade

bushwhacker

cavalry

confederacy

draft

dysentery

jayhawker

kepi

repeater

slavery

sovereignty

Yankee

Civil War Word Search Definitions

Abolitionist: a person who is against slavery

Antietam: the site of the bloodiest day of battle in the Civil War

Appomattox: the location where General Lee surrendered to General Grant

Assassination: the fate of President Lincoln immediately after the war

Bayonet: a long blade attached to a rifle barrel

Blockade: Union ships preventing trade in southern sea ports

Bushwhacker: a pro-slavery raider

Cavalry: soldiers mounted on horses

Confederacy: short for Confederate States of America

Draft: law requiring men to enlist in the armed forces

Dysentery: an illness that killed many Civil War soldiers

Jayhawker: an anti-slavery raider

Kepi: small rounded cap worn by soldiers

Repeater: a new kind of rifle used in the Civil War

Slavery: ownership of African Americans for use as unpaid labor

Sovereignty: the right of states to govern themselves as independent entities

Yankee: slang term for a Union soldier

War by the Numbers

Numbers and statistics can help tell the story of the War Between the States. Use classroom and media center resources to find the numbers and fill in the blanks below.

Note: Sources vary on these numbers. To support your findings, note the source for each answer.

1.   How many soldiers (total) fought in the war? _____

2.   What was the average age of a Civil War soldier? _____

3.   How many Union soldiers active in the war were under 18 years old? _____

4.   What single event and day of the war produced the most casualties? _____ _____ How many were killed or wounded in battle that day? _____

5.   How many Union soldiers died in battle in the Civil War? _____

6.   How many Union soldiers died of related causes (mainly disease) in the Civil War? _____

7.   How many Union soldiers were wounded in the war? _____

8.   How many Confederate soldiers died in the war? _____

9.   How many Confederate soldiers were wounded in the war? _____

10.   What percent of African American soldiers who fought for the Union died in battle or from related causes? _____

11.   Which Civil War prison camp had the worst record for saving the lives of its prisoners?

_____

12.   What was the total death toll of the Civil War? _____

13.   Circle the correct answer: The total number of American soldiers who died in the Civil War is

a) less than   b) equal to   c) more than   those killed in all other wars combined.

14.   From your research, compose a summary statement about the casualties from the American Civil War.

_____

_____

_____

War by the Numbers
Teacher Resource

Numbers and statistics can help tell the story of the War Between the States. Use classroom and media center resources to find the numbers and fill in the blanks below.

Note: Sources vary on these numbers. Allow for a range of answers, as long as students can cite their source information.

1. How many soldiers (total) fought in the war? **3,000,000**

2. What was the average age of a Civil War soldier? **21**

3. How many Union soldiers active in the war were under 18 years old? **800,000**

4. What single event and day of the war produced the most casualties? **Battle at Antietam Creek Sept. 17, 1862** How many were killed or wounded in battle that day? **24,000**

5. How many Union soldiers died in battle in the Civil War? **67,000**

6. How many Union soldiers died of related causes (mainly disease) in the Civil War? **268,000**

7. How many Union soldiers were wounded in the war? **275,000**

8. How many Confederate soldiers died in the war? **260,000**

9. How many Confederate soldiers were wounded in the war? **100,000**

10. What percent of African American soldiers who fought for the Union died in battle or from related causes? **22%**

11. Which Civil War prison camp had the worst record for saving the lives of its prisoners? **Camp Sumter at Andersonville, GA, lost more than 11,000 of 17,875 sick Union soldiers treated.**

12. What was the total death toll of the Civil War? **623,000**

13. Circle the correct answer: The total number of American soldiers who died in the Civil War is **a) less than** b) equal to c) more than those killed in all other wars combined.

14. From your research, compose a summary statement about the casualties from the American Civil War. **Answers will vary.**

Industrialization, City Life and World War I

The period from 1880–1929 saw huge changes in America. Cities swelled with the arrival of unprecedented numbers of immigrants from Europe and Asia, compounding both the enrichment and the challenges of blending diverse elements into one society. An explosion of new inventions advanced technology in all areas of manufacture, transportation, communications, entertainment, etc. The need for cheap labor and the appearance of the "robber baron" industrial capitalists highlighted the contrast between the "haves" and "have-nots" and inspired movements to unionize workers and end child labor. Women campaigned for and won the right to vote. The young country's involvement in the Spanish-American War and World War I thrust it onto the global stage as an emerging world power. And the brief emotional and economic honeymoon following World War I produced the unforgettable period of Prohibition, the Roaring Twenties and "glamorized gangsters," in all its drama and blissful unawareness of hard times to come.

Some themes of this period to explore through literature include:

★ A nation of immigrants.

★ Technological advances: Manufacturing, communications and transportation.

★ The labor movement and child labor.

★ Life, culture and entertainment in the cities.

★ Women's suffrage movement.

★ World War I: Emergence of a new world power.

★ Heroes, leaders and famous figures.

Additional series that might enrich your exploration include:

★ The American Girls Collection ("Welcome to Samantha's World" titles). Pleasant Company Publications. 4–5.

★ Cornerstones of Freedom. Children's Press. 4–7.

★ Cultures of America. Benchmark Books. 5–8.

Resources on Industrialization, City Life and World War I

★ Fiction

★ **After the Dancing Days** by Margaret I. Rostkowski. HarperCollins, 1988. 5–8. When 13-year-old Annie's father returns from the Great War he leaves his prestigious medical practice to treat wounded soldiers, much to the dismay of his family and community who just want to forget the war. Annie is drawn into friendship with a wounded, bitter young man who challenges her view of the realities of war and heroism. Watching their friendship develop not only educates the reader about the times, but also spotlights lingering attitudes toward war veterans.

★ **The Boxer** by Kathleen Karr. Farrar, Straus and Giroux, 2000. 6–8. Fifteen-year-old Johnny finds himself the man of the house after his father deserts the family. He discovers he's good with his fists and sets out to make his fortune and secure a better life for his family as a boxer. Lots of fight action is interspersed with description of tenement life in late-nineteenth-century New York City in this story full of determination and heart.

★ **Dave at Night** by Gail Carson Levine. HarperCollins, 2001. 5–7. Spunky, trouble-prone Dave is devastated when his father dies and relatives ship him off to the Hebrew Home for Boys. There he faces terrible conditions and the wrath of the abusive superintendent. He begins to sneak out at night and discovers the whole other world of the Harlem Renaissance, which welcomes him. With help from friends, both inside and outside the orphanage, Dave finds a real home for himself and a better life for his orphan buddies.

★ **Dragonwings** by Laurence Yep. Econo-Clad, 1989. 6–8. Newbery Honor Book. In 1903, at age eight, Moon Shadow leaves China to join his father in America. He helps in the laundry and finds his place in the Company, a group of men helping each other as family in a new land. With Moon Shadow, we are drawn into his father's dreams of flying like the Wright Brothers. Incidents of discrimination, unlikely friendships, deep loyalty, honor betrayed and fulfilled and compelling charac-

ters that challenge stereotypes make the book an important and satisfying read.

★ **Fair Weather** by Richard Peck. Dial Books for Young Readers, 2001. 5–8. This sweet, funny, adventure-packed novel is sure to become an American classic. Set at the Chicago World's Columbian Exposition of 1893, it reveals turn-of-the-century wonders as seen through the unsophisticated eyes of the Beckett children and their surprisingly worldly grandfather. Delightful characters, cameo appearances by celebrities of the day and rollicking humor make this pure pleasure. A great read-aloud title.

★ **Good-bye Billy Radish** by Gloria Skurzynski. Simon & Schuster, 1996. 6–8. Billy Radish (an Americanization of his Ukrainian name) and Hank Kerner are best friends. They live in a steel mill town during World War I, which forms the context for their evolving ideas about citizenship, heroism, love and family. The sometimes-harsh story evokes timeless joys and sorrows of family and friendship, while exploring issues of developing culture, the immigrant experience, the dangers of the mill and the deadly flu epidemic of 1918.

★ **The Jazz Kid** by James Lincoln Collier. Puffin Books, 1996. 6–8. Twelve-year-old Paulie is a goner! One taste of jazz, and all he wants to do with his life is play this music. His obsession causes him to flunk out of school, gets him in deep trouble at home and finally involves him in 1920s-Chicago speakeasies and organized crime. There is much to discover here about city life, early jazz, gangsters, nurturing talent, race relations and family bonds. The lessons are made palatable through lively text and well-drawn, sympathetic characters.

★ **Peppe the Lamplighter** by Elisa Bartone. William Morrow & Co., 1997. 4–6. Caldecott Honor Book. Young Italian immigrant Peppe must work to help his struggling siblings and sick father. He finds a job lighting street lamps and perseveres in spite of his father's scorn for his lowly task. Finally, a crisis proves the value of Peppe's work and earns him his father's respect and pride.

★ **Polar, the Titanic Bear** by Daisy Corning Stone Spedden. Little, Brown, 2001. 4–6. Spedden, real-life mother of the boy who was Master to the stuffed bear Polar, wrote this story for her son from the bear's point of view. It tells of an extremely privileged life, as well as surviving the Titanic disaster. An interesting story in itself, it clearly demonstrates the contrast between the rich and poor in early-twentieth-century America.

★ **Radio Rescue** by Lynne Barasch. Farrar, Straus and Giroux, 2000. 4–7. ALSC Notable Children's Book. Barasch's father was the youngest licensed ham radio operator in the U.S. in the early 1920s. She bases her story on his experiences. The young operator overhears an SOS message during a hurricane in Florida and puts his new skills to use, rousing the Coast Guard to rescue a stranded family. Along the way, the reader gets a quick education in Morse code, phone services and amateur radio operation.

★ **When Jessie Came Across the Sea** by Amy Hest. Candlewick Press, 1997. 4–8. The rabbi in 13-year-old Jessie's eastern European village decides she must go to America. She hates to leave her beloved grandmother, but can't disobey. Hest relates Jessie's journey by ship, her entrance through Ellis Island and her life as a seamstress and lace maker. The story reaches a sweet conclusion, as Jessie manages to bring her grandmother to America for her wedding. Rich, evocative illustrations and engaging text flesh out an appealing main character.

Nonfiction

★ **Coming Home: From the Life of Langston Hughes** by Floyd Cooper. Putnam, 1997. 4–6. Soft, lyrical illustrations draw the reader into the world of a young dreamer. Langston Hughes's longing for a real home, love for stories of black heroes and attraction to the jazzy street rhythms of Kansas City led him toward his role as a leader of the Harlem Renaissance of the 1920s and '30s and foremost African American poet of his time.

★ **Coming to America: The Story of Immigration** by Betsy Maestro. Scholastic, 1996. 4–8. Maestro makes the case that all Americans are, ultimately, immigrants and summarizes the history of immigration to this land from prehistory to the present. Because she is not restricted to one story, she can focus on the bigger picture. She points out familiar patterns of hardship for new immigrants, calls on us to recognize the achievements of each element of our immigrant population and reminds us to honor each other, recognizing our similarities and celebrating our diversity. A good tool for perspective.

★ **Immigrant Kids** by Russell Freedman. Econo-Clad, 1995. 5–8. Using photos and primary source material, Freedman examines the lives of immigrant children around the turn of the century in all their excitement, squalor, opportunities, harsh realities and promise. In effect, he tracks the experiences of a generation, a few of whom are still alive today.

★ **Kids at Work: Lewis Hine and the Crusade against Child Labor** by Russell Freedman. Econo-Clad, 1998. 5–8. Freedman tells the story of Lewis Hine, teacher-turned-photographer who dedicated much of his life to educating the public about the evils of child labor through his photos. The sincere, readable text teams up with Hine's photos to produce a powerful impact that should make children's eyes widen and inspire appreciation for the legacy of his efforts.

★ **The Progressive Years: 1901 to 1933** by Rose Blue and Corinne J. Naden. Raintree Steck-Vaughn, 1998. 5–8. This entertaining, informative Who's That in the White House? series title explores the lives and administrations of the men who served as president in the early 1900s. Varied illustrations support the text, which does a creditable job of summarizing and evaluating these complex men. Short sketches of people in the news and highlights from each administration add research value. For similar treatment of the late-nineteenth-century presidents, see the previous series title, *The Expansion Years: 1857 to 1901*.

★ **The Story of the Statue of Liberty** by Betsy and Giulio Maestro. Econo-Clad, 1989. 4–8. The Maestros again provide a rich and deceptively simple account of an important topic in U.S. history, in concise text and colorful illustrations. End matter provides additional facts about Lady Liberty, including a feature on Emma Lazarus and her famous poem inscribed on the statue's base.

★ **Streets of Gold** by Rosemary Wells. Dial Books for Young Readers, 1999. 4–8. Mary Antin and her family left Russia for the U.S. in 1894. She is known for a poem she wrote at age 13, as a new immigrant, that was printed in the Boston newspaper, and for a book about her experiences written later. This picture book biography relates events from her life in a Jewish settlement in Russia to her Boston tenement home and school. Lovely, warm paintings and an author's note support the clear, insightful text.

★ **Victorian Days: Discover the Past with Fun Projects, Games, Activities and Recipes** by David C. King. John Wiley & Sons, Inc., 2000. 4–7. This American Kids in History title, like its sister title listed in the Colonial America chapter, offers a wide range of interesting activities as it explores the period (specifically the year 1893) through the lives of fictional American families. Added interest comes from the fact that one family is made up of poor Polish immigrants and the other is that of a wealthy businessman. Again, the biggest drawback is the frequent reference to having adult help, which limits appeal to older students.

★ **You Want Women to Vote, Lizzie Stanton?** by Jean Fritz. Penguin Putnam Books for Young Readers, 1999. 4–6. With characteristic frankness and humor, Fritz paints a word portrait of the famous women's suffrage activist who, while shocking many and alienating some potential supporters with her radical ideas and actions, still did as much for women's rights as anyone. Much of Stanton's work was done before 1880, but she stayed active in the movement until her death in 1902.

Other Media

★ **The Complete Works of Scott Joplin** performed by Richard Zimmerman. Laserlight Piano Digital, 1993 (CD). 4–8. Any volume of this multivolume set will give students a taste of Joplin's brilliant, toe-tapping ragtime and other compositions. Biographical notes will help students understand how extraordinary Joplin's achievements were in the context of his time. The music is as appealing and infectious today as ever.

★ **The Great Inventors** by Lee Mendelson and Bill Melendez. Paramount Pictures, 1996 (videocassette). 4-6. This appealing video, featuring the familiar Peanuts characters as students presenting school reports, highlights the creations of American inventors and focuses on the work of Alexander Graham Bell, Thomas Edison and Henry Ford. A This is America, Charlie Brown series title.

★ **The Great War: An Evocation in Music and Drama through Recordings Made at the Time.** Pearl, 1993 (CD). 4-8. Recordings of World War I music are difficult to find. This one is available through Amazon.com, and features familiar war songs ("Over There" and "It's a Long Way to Tipperary") along with popular songs of the time ("Pack up Your Troubles" and "How Ya Gonna Keep 'Em Down on the Farm?").

Web sites

★ **National Archives and Records Administration: The Woman Suffrage Movement**
www.nara.gov/education/teaching/woman/home.html

★ **The Roaring Twenties Net Activities**
www.mcdougallittell.com/whist/netact/U7/U7left.htm

★ **Turn-of-the-Century America: Photographs from the Detroit Publishing Company 1880–1920**
lcweb2.loc.gov/detroit/dethome.html *(Check out Activities on the Learning Page)*

Resources on Industrialization, City Life and World War I

★ Discussion Prompts

Use these prompts to stimulate discussion of themes and issues of the period.

★ **Appreciating Inventions.** If it is age appropriate, start by watching *The Great Inventors*. Have the class discuss how their daily lives would be different without the following inventions, which came into use during the period from 1880–1929:

- light bulb
- telephone
- amusement park
- radio and television
- motion picture camera
- automobile
- electric elevator
- hamburger, carbonated soft drinks and potato chips
- airplane
- basketball

★ **"Haves" and "Have-nots."** The contrast between America's wealthy and poor became increasingly clear during this period, and resulting tensions and resentments grew and found expression in such things as the labor movement and campaigns to limit immigration. As a way to approach this still painful and unresolved aspect of life in America, read *Polar, the Titanic Bear, Peppe the Lamplighter* and *When Jessie Came Across the Sea*. You might also compare and contrast the two families depicted in *Victorian Days,* or Dave's life with that of his high society friends in *Dave at Night*. Then use these prompts to discuss the issue.

- Compare the shipboard experiences of Jessie (*When Jessie Came Across the Sea*) and Douglas (*Polar, the Titanic Bear*)—before the Titanic's tragic accident, of course!

- Compare Douglas's home and family life to that of Peppe. What similarities can you see? What differences?

- Which family do you think arrived in the U.S. earlier? Explain your answer.

- How do you think Peppe would feel about Douglas and his privileged life?

- How do you think Douglas would feel about the conditions and hardships of Peppe's life?

- Could these two boys have been friends? How could they have learned from and helped each other?

- Are there equally dramatic contrasts today between the lives of the rich and poor in America? Is it only new immigrant families that tend to be poor and long-established families that tend to be rich?

- What problems in America and the world today have their roots in these extremes of wealth and poverty?

★ **The Promise of Liberty.** In *The Story of the Statue of Liberty*, we learn that the statue was a gift from France to the U.S., celebrating America's love of freedom and welcoming attitude toward immigrants wanting to share in that freedom. Read with the class the famous Emma Lazarus poem, "The New Colossus." It discusses the promise of welcome implied in the poem and embodied in the statue.

- What does Lady Liberty promise to poor and oppressed people of the world?

- How does that promise relate to our laws and attitudes toward immigrants today?

- Have we, as a nation, kept that promise?

★ Games

★ **Turn-of-the-Century Matching Game.** Have students match the names of well-known figures from around the turn of the century (1900) to their role or identity. See reproducible handout on page 60.

★ **Presidential Bingo.** Use the reproducible handout on page 61 to play this game. Adjust the time investment and challenge level by

assigning it to individuals or teams, and by requiring students to complete either a vertical, horizontal or diagonal row or the entire sheet to win. Give students a limited amount of time to use appropriate resources to find the answers and fill out their bingo sheets. The first student or team to identify the required number of presidents correctly is the winner. All answers can be found in *The Progressive Years* and its sister volume mentioned in the bibliography, but should be available in any basic reference collection.

★ **Pebble Target Game.** In *Victorian Days,* we learn that many Americans made up versions of outdoor games to play indoors during this period. To make the game, you will need:

> several sheets of newspaper
>
> 5 clean tuna fish or cat food cans with only the tops removed
>
> pencil
>
> ruler
>
> 1 to 2 sheets of wrapping paper or construction paper
>
> scissors
>
> white glue
>
> marking pen, black or red
>
> pine board or thick cardboard, about 12-by-24 inches
>
> 5 thumbtacks
>
> hammer
>
> 5 pebbles or dried beans for each player, and some extras
>
> adult helper

- Spread the newspaper on your work surface and place the 5 empty cans on top.

- With pencil and ruler, measure strips of paper to fit around the outside of each can. Cut out the strips and fix them to the cans with white glue as shown below.

- Use the marking pen to write the number 5 on the inside bottom of four of the cans and a 10 on the fifth can.

- Arrange the cans on the board or cardboard with the 10-point target in the center.

- With an adult's help, use a hammer to tack the target cans in place. The sides of the four outer targets should touch the center target. Prop your target board against a piece of furniture or a stack of books.

To play:

- Two or three can play individually; if four play, divide into two teams. Use any method you wish to see who goes first.

- Practice a few times to establish a comfortable tossing line—a distance that makes scoring possible, but not too easy. Use extra pebbles to mark the line; once the line is marked, no player can cross it or reach over it.

- Players take turns, with each player having 5 tosses. Fifty points are needed to win a round. If no one has 50 points after a round, the scores carry over to the next round.

Artistic/Creative Expressions

★ **Diorama.** Have students choose scenes from their favorite books in this chapter, and create shoebox dioramas illustrating the action.

★ **Letters to the Editor.** Based on their reading, have students imagine themselves living during this period in American history. Assign them to choose a social issue from the time that interests them and to write a letter to the editor of the local newspaper explaining and defending their views on the issue. To sharpen the challenge, you might instruct students to research the main arguments of those who opposed their views and refute them in their letters. Here are some sample topics:

- Why women should be granted the right to vote.

- Why child labor should be outlawed.

- Why we should remember and honor veterans of war.

- Why women should give up corsets and wear bloomers.

- Why companies should not be allowed to force their employees to buy only from the company store.

- Why and how the number of immigrants entering America should be controlled.

★ **Book Talks.** Assign older students to read *The Boxer; Good-bye, Billy Radish; After the Dancing Days; The Jazz Kid; Dragonwings; Dave at Night* or *Fair Weather*. Students will prepare brief (one to two minute) talks for the class, designed to entice others to read the book. Book talks are similar to oral book reports, but may be less complete and analytical and more entertaining. They often end with a cliff-hanger. For a fun follow-up activity, poll the class to see who plans to read which book, based on which book talk.

Practical Crafts

★ **Deviled Eggs.** In *Fair Weather,* Rosie reflects that city people who got their eggs by train from the country "had never tasted a fresh egg in their lives and didn't even know it." Still, eggs were a favorite and a staple in both country and city kitchens. Stuffed eggs had been around for a long time, but in the late 1800s people began to spice them up with hot seasonings, earning them the new name, "Deviled eggs." Make this recipe for a treat that is still popular today. Have students work in teams of six. You might let students experiment with different spices and seasonings to "devil" their eggs, then share and compare. The ingredients you will need are:

    6 shelled, hard-boiled eggs

    4 tablespoons mayonnaise

    1 teaspoon minced onion

    ½ teaspoon prepared mustard

    Salt, pepper, cayenne pepper, chili powder, dill weed or other spices to taste

- Cut hard-boiled eggs in half the long way. Carefully remove yolks to a bowl and mash them. Add remaining ingredients to mashed yolks and mix well. Spoon filling back into egg whites. Chill them in the refrigerator for an hour, covered with wax paper, before eating.

★ **Sand-Dried Flowers.** New immigrant families found many different ways for members to contribute to the family income. Mary, from the Kadinsky family in *Victorian Days,* learned to dry flowers to be arranged for sale by a neighborhood street vendor. To make them, you will need:

8 to 12 flowers with thick blossoms (roses, mums, carnations, etc., work well)

scissors

several sheets of newspaper

piece of string

2 pails of clean sand

small, sturdy box with lid (a shoe box is perfect), or an old cookie tin

sand shovel or large spoon

toothpick

masking tape

small paintbrush

green florist's wire (available at craft and hobby stores)

3 to 4 sprigs of rosemary, baby's breath, lavender or heather (available at florist shops)

paper lace doily, 6 to 8 inches in diameter 18-inch piece of ½-inch ribbon

- Try to pick your flowers on a dry, sunny day. Cut a few inches of stem and some leaves as well. If the blossoms are wet, let them dry before you work with them.

- Spread several sheets of newspaper on your work surface and place the flowers on top.

- Cut the stems 1½ to 2 inches below each blossom. Tie the leftover stems and leaves in a bunch and hang them in a warm, dark place, like a closet, to dry for a week or two.

- Fill the bottom of the box with about 2 inches of sand. Place the blossoms in the sand with the stems down, except for flowers that have a radiating (or circle) blossom, like daisies or black-eyed Susans, which can be placed stem-side up.

- Carefully shovel sand over each blossom in between the petals. You want to get rid of any air pockets around the blossoms. Use a toothpick to push sand gently around and between the petals.

- Add enough sand to cover all the blossoms with about 1 inch of sand. Place the lid on the box and seal the edges with masking tape so that the box is airtight. (The tape isn't necessary if you're using a cookie tin.) Store the box in a warm, dry place for two weeks.

- After two weeks, remove the tape and the lid. Gently uncover one blossom to test it. If the petals feel dry, like paper, the flowers are ready; if not, replace the lid and allow an additional few days for drying.

- When the blossoms are dry, carefully remove them from the sand. Handle them by the stems as much as possible, since the petals will be quite brittle. Use a small paintbrush to brush off any leftover sand.

- Untie the string from the stems and leaves. Use a short piece of florist's wire to attach a stem and a leaf or two to each blossom. Arrange several of the blossoms with a sprig or two of lavender, baby's breath or other filler.

- Form the doily into a cone shape with your bouquet inside. Wrap the bottom of the doily around the stems, then tie it firmly with a piece of ribbon 5 or 6 inches long. Tie one end of a 12-inch piece of ribbon to the top of the doily cone by threading the ribbon through a hole in the doily, then tying a knot at the back. Tie the other end to the opposite side of the cone, as shown. Use this ribbon loop to hang the bouquet from a tack on the wall, or from the edge of a mirror or picture.

★ **Tea Biscuits.** Here's a quick and easy way to make tasty Tea Biscuits, a favorite for tea parties. Of course, in earlier times, they would have made the sweet dough from scratch. Follow the shortcake recipe on the box of a standard baking mix like Bisquick or Jiffy. Roll the dough ½" thick. Cut with cookie cutters. Before baking, push a deep hollow into the center of each biscuit. While the biscuits bake, mix a package of instant lemon pudding. Drop a dollop of lemon pudding in the hollow of each baked biscuit. Alternatively, you can place a spoonful of fruit jam or preserves in the hollow of each biscuit before baking.

★ **Color Tea.** Students can pretend to be "high society" by preparing a Color Tea for the class. This was popular in the early 1900s and is something Aunt Euterpe, in *Fair Weather*, or Douglas Spedden's mother from *Polar, the Titanic Bear* might have done. A Color Tea was a fancy tea party with everything planned around the chosen color—invitations, table settings, food, even the guests' clothing, when possible. You have the beginnings of a Yellow Color Tea already, with deviled eggs and lemon tea biscuits. Add lemonade and finger sandwiches made with yellow cheese; find a yellow tablecloth, plates and centerpiece flowers, and you're ready to go!

★ Research Projects

Invite students to use these opportunities to explore the period from 1880–1929 as individual or small group projects, or involve the whole class.

★ **Your Immigrant Community.** Start by reviewing *Coming to America*. Have the class research the geography, history and customs of the main countries of origin of families in your community. Find out what brought immigrants here from those countries, when they came and what work they found. Identify leaders in the community from each national background. You might assign a team to explore each country. Students should present oral reports of their findings, using maps and other visuals to illustrate. You could conclude this activity by inviting a recent immigrant to visit the class and share his or her experiences of adjustment and nationalization.

★ **Mining Classroom Talent.** Each student will choose a real-life person from the period that shares an interest or talent with the student. For example, a student interested in music might pick Scott Joplin, Louis Armstrong or Lillian Russell; a student interested in science might choose one of the inventors, etc. The matching game on page 60 could be used as a starting list of people to consider. After choosing, each student will research independently to complete the three phases of the assignment.

- Learn about the person's life and write a brief (one page) biography.

- Study the person's accomplishments or creations and summarize them for the class using visuals, recordings, etc., as appropriate.

- Prepare and present something of your own based on the interest or talent shared with the person. For example, a would-be writer might share an original poem in honor of Mary Antin or Langston Hughes. A student researching George Eastman might show photographs he or she took. A fan of Thomas Edison might demonstrate an invention of his or her own. An aspiring social activist might study Susan B. Anthony or Lewis Hine, and share a personal plan of action to address an injustice in the community.

Encourage students to be creative! Costumes and theatrics might be part of this mining of classroom talent.

★ **Labor Issues, Then and Now.** Use the reproducible worksheet on page 63 to help students explore laws and conditions pertaining to laborers. Using titles from the bibliography (the Russell Freedman titles are excellent sources) and other classroom or media center resources, students should find at least one quotation or summary statement about each of the bubble items in the web for circa 1900 and the present day. An example is given. After collecting the worksheets, you might assemble students' findings onto a chart that compares labor issues and conditions then and now, to review with the class.

Turn-of-the-Century Figures Matching Game

Draw a line from the names of these well-known turn-of-the-century figures in the first column to their roles or identities in the second column.

Mary Antin

teacher of the deaf who invented the telephone

Woodrow Wilson

Russian Jewish immigrant who became known as a writer

Scott Joplin

photographer who campaigned against child labor

Annie Oakley

African American ragtime musician

Teddy Roosevelt

popular actress and singer

Lillian Russell

American president known as "Rough Rider" and "Teddy Bear"

George Eastman

famous activist for women's suffrage

Alexander Graham Bell

businessman and inventor best known for inventing the easy-to-use box camera

Lewis Hine

famous capitalist and philanthropist

Orville Wright

sharp shooter in Wild West shows

Andrew Carnegie

American president and chief planner of the League of Nations

Susan B. Anthony

one of the brothers who made the first successful flight in a powered airplane

Presidential Bingo Game

Use classroom or media center resources to answer the questions in the bingo squares below. Indicate your answer by writing the initials of the appropriate president across the square in colored marker or crayon.

James Garfield (JG)   William McKinley (WM)   Warren G. Harding (WH)
Chester A. Arthur (CA)   Theodore Roosevelt (TR)   Calvin Coolidge (CC)
Grover Cleveland (GC)   William H. Taft (WT)   Herbert Hoover (HH)
Benjamin Harrison (BH)   Woodrow Wilson (WW)

in office when women won the vote	Teddy Bear named after him	thought up the League of Nations	married while in office (more than one right answer)	"Keep cool with ____ ."
youngest man elected president up to that time	president during World War I	wanted to be a Supreme Court justice	president when the Statue of Liberty was dedicated	declared war on Spain
married in the White House	elected to a later term after being defeated as incumbent	★ FREE	biggest man, physically, ever elected president	assassinated while in office
had White House redecorated before moving in	brought a pet kangaroo to the White House	his grandfather was president before him	in office when the stock market crashed in 1929	in office when Native Americans were given citizenship
supervised relief efforts after World War I	admitted six states during his administration	campaigned for "a return to normalcy"	legal advocate of African Americans' rights before becoming president	administration plagued by corruption scandals (two possible answers)

Presidential Bingo Game
Teacher Resource

Use the resource below to check the class Bingo cards.

James Garfield (JG)　　William McKinley (WM)　　Warren G. Harding (WH)
Chester A. Arthur (CA)　　Theodore Roosevelt (TR)　　Calvin Coolidge (CC)
Grover Cleveland (GC)　　William H. Taft (WT)　　Herbert Hoover (HH)
Benjamin Harrison (BH)　　Woodrow Wilson (WW)

in office when women won the vote (WW)	Teddy Bear named after him (TR)	thought up the League of Nations (WW)	married while in office (more than one right answer) (WW or GC)	"Keep cool with _____ ." (CC)
youngest man elected president up to that time (TR)	president during World War I (WW)	wanted to be a Supreme Court justice (WT)	president when the Statue of Liberty was dedicated (GC)	declared war on Spain (WM)
married in the White House (GC)	elected to a later term after being defeated as incumbent (GC)	FREE	biggest man, physically, ever elected president (WT)	assassinated while in office (JG)
had White House redecorated before moving in (CA)	brought a pet kangaroo to the White House (TR)	his grandfather was president before him (BH)	in office when the stock market crashed in 1929 (HH)	in office when Native Americans were given citizenship (CC)
supervised relief efforts after World War I (HH)	admitted six states during his administration (BH)	campaigned for "a return to normalcy" (WH)	legal advocate of African Americans' rights before becoming president (CA)	administration plagued by corruption scandals (two possible answers) (WH or CC)

Labor Issues and Conditions "Then and Now" Web

Use books from the chapter bibliography and other classroom or media center resources to find a quotation or write a summary statement about each of the items in the web for circa 1900 and the present day. See the example below.

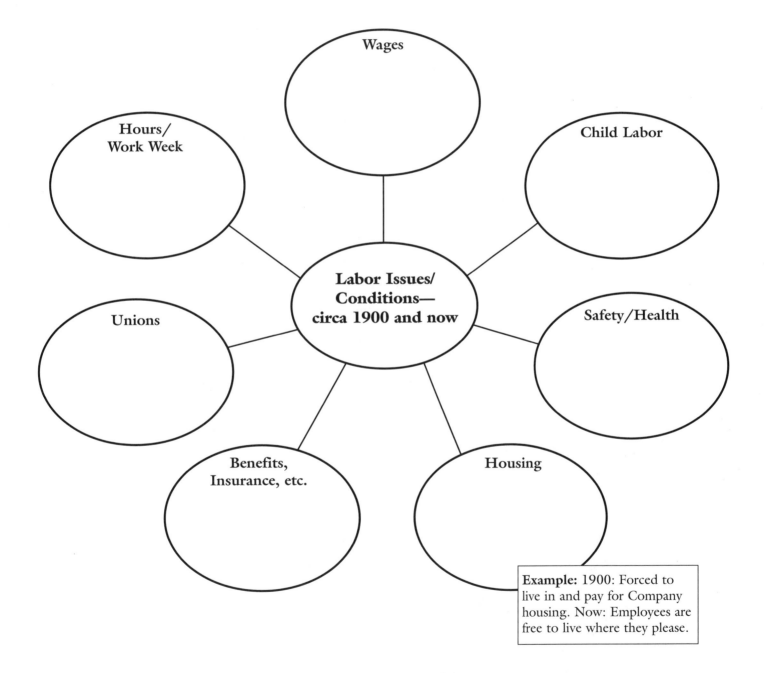

Wages

Hours/ Work Week

Child Labor

Unions

Labor Issues/ Conditions— circa 1900 and now

Safety/Health

Benefits, Insurance, etc.

Housing

Example: 1900: Forced to live in and pay for Company housing. Now: Employees are free to live where they please.

The Great Depression

When the stock market crashed in October 1929, it threw the whole country into shock. Whether lulled by postwar good feelings or worn down by ongoing economic hardships in the country's farming communities and poor neighborhoods, few Americans saw the warning signs. Fortunes were lost overnight in the spectacular start of what was to be a deep 12-year depression felt throughout the entire industrialized world. To make matters worse, a severe and relentless drought moved across the country and settled in the Great Plains. Not only would crops not grow from Montana and the Dakotas to Texas for much of the 1930s, but unwise agricultural practices had stripped the land of trees and plants needed to anchor the soil, which blew away in furious dust storms that sickened people and deepened their poverty. Large segments of the population became transient, following the promise of work wherever it was rumored to be. Migrant labor camps and "riding the rails" became ways of life for the poorest of the poor, while the cities' missions doled out bread and "depression soup" to multitudes of needy residents.

While Hoover was largely blamed for poor leadership in the crisis, his successor, Franklin Delano Roosevelt, was beloved as a man of action who brought hope and some improvement to the nation. Through his "New Deal," Roosevelt changed forever the way the federal government involves itself in the economic life of the American people. In the end, however, it was only the economic boost of World War II that moved the U.S. and its fellow sufferers in Europe out of the depression and back toward prosperity.

Some themes of this period to explore through literature include:

★ Causes of the depression and the dust bowl.

★ "Making do," getting along day to day.

★ Looking for work—transients on the move.

★ Roosevelt and the changing role of government.

★ Escaping the gloom through recreation and entertainment.

★ Gains and losses in conditions of women, laborers and minorities.

These series might enrich your exploration:

★ Black Americans of Achievement. Chelsea House Publishers. 6–8.

★ The Drama of American History by Christopher Collier and James Lincoln Collier. Benchmark Books. 5–8.

Resources on the Great Depression

★ Fiction

★ ***Bud, Not Buddy*** by Christopher Paul Curtis. Delacorte Press, 1999. 5–8. Newbery Medal Book, ALSC Notable Children's Book. Bud has been in and out of the orphanage since his Momma died. After bad experiences with foster homes, he lights out to look for the man he's convinced is his father. His journey takes him through the world of soup lines, jazz, hobo shantytowns, unionization efforts, segregation and the poverty of the Depression, on his way to finding a place to belong. Lots of good period detail supports engaging characters in this satisfying story.

★ ***Cat Running*** by Zilpha Keatley Snyder. Bantam Doubleday Dell Books for Young Readers, 1996. 5–7. Cat's struggles with her family cause her to explore the creek, where she makes a secret place in a grotto. When she finds her retreat invaded, and by a dirty "Okie" child from shantytown at that, she is furious. But gradually Cat befriends the child and her family. Through that friendship, and a crisis that endangers the child's life, Cat learns about tolerance, friendship and dignity.

★ ***Dust for Dinner*** by Ann Turner. HarperCollins, 1995. 4–5. This advanced reader follows Jake and Maggy's family as they lose their farm during dust bowl days and head to California to find work. Dust blizzards, farm auctions and tent camps for transients are all part of the hard times before Papa finds a new job.

★ ***Fire on the Wind*** by Linda Crew. Econo-Clad, 1997. 6–8. When Storie's grandfather was logging, it seemed the trees would last forever. Her father believes they will, but as Storie sees the results of clear-cutting on the land and animals, she wonders. Then comes the summer of 1933, with severe drought creating tinderbox conditions in Oregon's forests. Crew gives us an involving and personal story of the impact of the Tillamook Burn on one young woman coming of age, as well as a glimpse of environmental issues and gender roles in the 1930s.

★ ***The Gardener*** by Sarah Stewart. Farrar, Straus and Giroux, 2000. 4–5. During the depression, Papa and Mama can't find work. Lydia Grace goes to the city to help in her uncle's bakery until things improve. While she hates to leave her family, she determines to make the best of things. Her story is told through letters she writes and extraordinary illustrations which convey details and evoke emotions of the period. Lydia Grace gives new meaning to the adage, "Bloom where you're planted."

★ ***The Gawgon and the Boy*** by Lloyd Alexander. Dutton Children's Books, 2001. 5–7. Details of depression life form the context for this witty, wonderful story. David (the Boy) is tutored by his eccentric aunt (the Gawgon) while recovering from an illness. She shares an exciting world of books and ideas that spark his interest as school never has before. Snippets of heroes and legendary drama mix with routine events of daily life and are transformed into wild, amusing, dreamlike fantasy adventures in his vivid imagination. When his aunt dies, David must find within himself ways to inspire his talents and build her wisdom into his life.

★ ***Ida Early Comes over the Mountain*** by Robert Burch. Viking Press, 1980. 4–8. Life is glum for the Sutton family, whose proper but cranky Aunt Ernestine is no match for the mother who died a few months ago. But then Ida Early shows up with her odd appearance and quirky mix of tall tales, surprising skills and undemanding affection. Through Ida and the reactions of others to her strangeness, the family learns what it means to have and to be true friends.

★ ***A Jar of Dreams*** by Yoshiko Uchida. Simon & Schuster, 1981. 4–7. Eleven-year-old Rinko wants to fit in, which isn't easy when you're Japanese and attending a white school in San Francisco during the depression. She isn't the only one experiencing prejudice. Her father's business fails, her mother's business is sabotaged by bigoted white competitors and white officials won't help. But then Aunt Waka visits from Japan, and her quiet strength and encouragement inspire everyone to stand proud and follow their dreams.

★ ***Leah's Pony*** by Elizabeth Friedrich. Boyds Mills Press, 1999. 4–6. When Leah's parents can't repay a bank loan during the depression, they arrange an auction to settle the debt. They know that if they lose the tractor, they will lose everything, including the farm. Leah sells her beloved pony, naively hoping to buy

the tractor at auction. Her sacrifice touches her neighbors, who pitch in to save the farm. An author's note explains about "penny auctions." A lovely, touching look at family and community solidarity.

★ ***A Letter to Mrs. Roosevelt*** by C. Coco De Young. Delacorte Press, 1999. 4–6. Based on a true story, this novel of one family's hardships during the depression has something special to offer. Eleven-year-old Margo shares her experiences of those hardships and also tunes into and shares the pain and frustration of her parents, for whom we come to feel as sympathetic as we do for the child. Margo responds to the threat of losing their home by writing to the First Lady for help. The response, and the manner of its delivery, adds a delightful twist to this lovely, sensitive story.

★ ***Mississippi Bridge*** by Mildred D. Taylor. Bantam, 1992. 4–6. Jeremy Simms is the son of a bigoted white tenant farmer, who doesn't share his father's prejudices. He witnesses an ugly confrontation in which black passengers are forced off a bus to make room for whites, and is thrown into anguish and confusion when the bus goes off a bridge in a storm, killing some passengers. The first rescuer to arrive is a black would-be passenger, fresh from the humiliating confrontation. A quick, easy read, this story packs a typical Taylor punch and gives younger readers much to think about.

★ ***Out of the Dust*** by Karen Hesse. Scholastic, 1997. 6–8. Newbery Medal Book, ALSC Notable Children's Book, Scott O'Dell Historical Fiction Award Book. Arranged by seasons, this deeply moving novel chronicles in poetry the dust bowl experiences of a farm girl from Oklahoma. Her dreams of music, adventure and normalcy are shattered by a fire that ruins her hands for piano, the death of her mother and newborn brother, her father's grief and despair and the seemingly endless dust. Slowly, painfully and eloquently hope emerges "out of the dust," born of self-knowledge, honesty and love.

★ ***Roll of Thunder, Hear My Cry*** by Mildred D. Taylor. Dial Books, 1976. 6–8. Newbery Medal Book. Taylor writes about the Logans, a landowning black family in Mississippi cotton country. Cassie and her brothers try to understand as the family struggles to keep their land at the height of the depression, and as tensions between blacks and whites escalate to terrifying levels of cruelty, injustice and violence. A brutally honest look at racial strife at

its ugliest and most complex, it still manages to hold out hope that honor and integrity, as portrayed by the Logans and their white lawyer friend, may eventually prevail.

★ ***Uncle Jed's Barbershop*** by Margaree King Mitchell. Simon & Schuster Books for Young Readers, 1993. 4–6. Sarah Jean's uncle dreams of owning a barbershop. The only black barber around, he travels to his customers' homes while he saves his money. Uncle Jed sees his dream nearly destroyed twice—once when he gives his savings to pay for Sarah Jean's surgery, and again when his bank fails in 1929. But he never gives up, and his resilience of spirit inspires many and compounds his joy when his dream comes true. A moving look at segregation, selflessness, hardship and loyalty.

★ ***When Willard Met Babe Ruth*** by Donald Hall. Harcourt Brace, 2001. 4–5. In a stroke of luck, 12-year-old Willard meets his idol, a young baseball player named Babe Ruth. Over the years, as Willard and his family struggle with farm life in the depression, they follow "The Babe's" career. A 1935 trip to a Boston Braves game brings Willard face-to-face again with the famous player, who is now his daughter's idol as well. A fun, easy read that celebrates both "the best who ever played the game" and the strength and love of family through hard times.

★ ***A Year Down Yonder*** by Richard Peck. Dial Books for Young Readers, 2000. 5–8. Newbery Medal Book, ALSC Notable Children's Book. This hilarious, quirky, charming sequel to *A Long Way From Chicago* (see Other Media section) is another Richard Peck triumph. During the depression, Mary Alice is appalled to have to spend a whole year with her outrageous, eccentric, embarrassing grandmother in small-town Illinois while her parents cope with joblessness. But the year turns out better than expected as Grandma deals with everyday events and major crises in unexpected ways and Mary Alice comes to appreciate her larger-than-life relative. Lots of period detail creates the context for this delight of a novel.

⭐ Nonfiction

★ ***Amelia Earhart: Aviation Pioneer*** by Roxane Chadwick. Lerner Publications, 1991. 4–6. This Earhart biography stands out for its brevity, clarity and completeness. Illustrated with lots of good black-and-white photos, it captures the spirit and the mystique of this fearless, unconventional woman.

★ *The FDR Way* by Jeffrey Morris. Lerner Publications, 1996. 5–8. This Great Presidential Decisions series title follows FDR's administration, providing global context and focusing on his major decisions about fighting the depression, establishing Social Security, getting involved in World War II and promoting the United Nations. The writing style is balanced, clear and accessible. Lots of good illustrations and sidebars add interest. An excellent look at America's role in the world during this turbulent time.

★ *Growing up in the Great Depression* by Richard Wormser. Atheneum, 1994. 6–8. Wormser summarizes the causes and major elements of the depression with frankness and balance. Chapters on hobos, the plains drought, work and labor issues, conditions for African Americans and women, the CCC, education and the experience of the rich give a broad view of what life was like for many growing up in this most challenging time. Good research value.

★ *Louis Armstrong: Musician* by Sam Tanenhaus. Holloway House, 1991. 7–8. Armstrong's career spanned several decades, but he was at the peak of his talent and creativity in the 1930s and the depression impacted him on many levels. The life and career, failings and setbacks, alongside genius and stunning successes, of this famous and beloved jazz musician make for fascinating reading and provide a commentary on his times. A Black Americans of Achievement series title.

★ *A Multicultural Portrait of the Great Depression* by Susan Rensberger. Benchmark Books, 1996. 6–8. A good overview of the Great Depression from the Perspectives series, this book emphasizes less-covered topics like the impact of the depression on arts and culture, gender and family roles and the depression experiences of specific ethnic groups.

★ *The Seventeenth Child* by Dorothy Marie Rice and Lucille Mabel Walthall Payne. Shoe String Press, 1998. 7–8. Mabel Walthall was the 17th child in a black sharecropper family, growing up during the depression. In brief anecdotes she shares memories of moving from place to place, of food and entertainment, working the tobacco fields, making

money and relationships with family and friends. A straightforward, unadorned account of the times.

★ *Will Rogers: Quotable Cowboy* by Cathereen L. Bennett. Runestone Press, 1995. 4–8. The dry-witted, free-spirited entertainer's story is shared in interesting text and black-and-white photos. His career, which included Wild West shows, stage, radio, print, television, silent movies and "talkies," provides a snapshot of the rapid development of the entertainment industry over a few decades. Rogers was the highest paid American movie star at the time of his death in the mid-1930s, and his wide appeal says much about the spirit of the period.

★ Other Media

★ *Hard Luck Blues* by Woody Guthrie. Catfish Records, 2001 (CD). 4–8. Guthrie, a pioneer in the field of using folk music to express the struggles of the working man, gives voice to many aspects of the 1930s including the depression and the dust bowl. The CD includes his famous celebration of America, "This Land Is Your Land," which may be familiar to students.

★ *Long Way from Chicago* by Richard Peck, read by Ron McLarty. Listening Library, 1999 (3 audiocassettes). Newbery Honor Book, ALSC Notable Children's Book. 5–8. An effective recording of this hilarious novel, made up of related but stand-alone short stories. Mary Alice and her brother, visiting from Chicago, become witnesses to Grandma Dowdle's incorrigible antics which keep things lively in her little town and often dispense a roundabout justice.

★ Web sites

★ *1930s Great Depression Gallery, Michigan Historical Museum*
www.sos.state.mi.us/history/museum/explore/museums/hismus/1900-75/depressn

★ *The American Experience: Riding the Rails*
www.pbs.org/wgbh/amex/rails

★ *Franklin Delano Roosevelt*
www.americanpresident.org/KoTrain/Courses/FDR/FDR_In_Brief.htm

★ *New Deal Network: The Great Depression, the 1930s and the Roosevelt Administration*
newdeal.feri.org

Activities on the Great Depression

★ Discussion Prompts

Use these prompts to stimulate discussion of themes and issues of the period.

★ **Causes and Results of the Depression.** Chapter one of *Growing up in the Great Depression* and chapter two of *A Multicultural Portrait of the Great Depression* analyze causes of the Great Depression. The poem "The Path of Our Sorrow," in *Out of the Dust,* offers Billie Jo's teacher's thoughts about the origins of the depression and the dust bowl crisis. Using these and other sources, lead a discussion of the causes of the economic hardships of the period. The following prompts may be helpful:

- What warning signs that the economy was in trouble could be found during the 1920s?

- Why didn't more people notice these signs and try to prevent economic collapse?

- What were the major causes of the Great Depression? (You might build on the "Haves" and "Have-nots" discussion from the previous chapter, exploring how extremes of wealth and poverty relate to the depression.)

- What practices of farmers and ranchers in the central plains made the effects of the droughts of the 1930s worse?

- How did the Great Depression change the relationship between the federal government and the people of the nation?

- What lessons do you think we learned from the depression and the dust bowl crises? What lessons do we still have to learn?

★ **"Nothing to Fear but Fear Itself."** In FDR's first inaugural address he told the people, "We have nothing to fear but fear itself— nameless, unreasoning, unjustified terror which paralyzes needed efforts to convert retreat into advance." Use these prompts to discuss his words with the class:

- Considering the condition of the country in March 1933, what do you think Roosevelt meant by these words?

- How did Roosevelt's confident call to courage and action help improve conditions in the country?

- The first part of this quotation has become famous and is often quoted. What new meaning might it have for Americans today?

★ **Gender Roles in the 1930s.** Based on the reading, discuss attitudes about appropriate roles and behavior for men and women, boys and girls in the 1930s. Call for examples from the books to support the ideas. *Cat Running, Fire on the Wind* and *A Multicultural Portrait of the Great Depression* are good sources. These prompts may help guide the discussion:

- What was considered proper clothing for boys and girls, men and women in the 1930s?

- What was considered "women's work?" "Men's work?" How hard was it for women to cross the line and do "men's work," and vice versa?

- What were the attitudes toward education for girls? For boys?

- Who were some of the courageous people who championed the rights of women, broke through gender stereotypes and helped to open up more choices for both women and men today?

★ Games

★ **Mystery Phrase Game.** Use the reproducible handout on page 71 to play this game. To make this easier for younger students, you might hand out copies of the word bank to use in filling in the blanks, or write the words on the board.

Answers:
1. sh(a)recroppers
2. E(l)eanor Roosevelt
3. car(d)board
4. Hoovervill(e)s
5. labor u(n)ions
6. dust bo(w)l
7. br(e)ad lines

Mystery phrase: New Deal

★ **"News Tag."** In *A Letter to Mrs. Roosevelt,* Margo mentions playing news tag with teacher-turned-grocer Mr. Frappa. Enjoy a round of Great Depression "News Tag." This is an open book activity, to have fun using what you've learned about the period from

1929–1941. Explain the game as follows: The first student called on will have a short time to come up with a phrase or sentence that could have been a newspaper headline during the period. Anything goes that demonstrates knowledge of the period. Give a couple of examples ("Louis Armstrong Plays at Local Nightclub," "Record Unemployment in the City," "FDR Elected Again!"). Once that student has produced an appropriate headline, he or she calls on another student and so on. Go through as many headlines as you wish. This game can be played in short bursts, as breaks from classroom routine.

★ **Monopoly!** Charles B. Darrow invented the game of Monopoly in 1934. He was unemployed and made 5,000 game sets by hand to sell. The game provided a much-needed fantasy escape into the world of wealth and easy living. By 1935, it was the best-selling game in the country!

★ Artistic/Creative Expressions

★ **Poems of Everyday Life.** Using *Out of the Dust* as example and inspiration, have students write their own poems about events and emotions of their everyday lives. Invite students to read their poems and share their thoughts about poetry as a form of personal expression.

★ **Character Conversations.** This chapter's books are full of interesting, appealing, real and fictional characters. This activity allows students to spend more time with these characters and build on what they have learned about the period. Arrange students in groups of three. You might assign these groups and the characters represented in each, or have students indicate favorite characters from the reading and then assign them in logical groupings with something in common. Try to include a real person from the period in each group. Then give each group a topic or question to discuss "in character." For example, one group might consist of Eleanor Roosevelt, Cassie from *Roll of Thunder, Hear My Cry* and Cat from *Cat Running*, discussing the need for better opportunities for poor people and minorities during the depression. Another might be Amelia Earhart, Uncle Jed from *Uncle Jed's Barbershop* and Rinko from *A Jar of Dreams*, talking about not giving up on your dreams. Will Rogers, Ida Early and Grandma Dowdel from *A Year Down Yonder* and *A Long Way from Chicago* might

share thoughts on laughing at yourself and finding fun in life. Louis Armstrong, Bud and Billie Jo from *Out of the Dust* might discuss what music means to them. Find your own combinations and topics, or have students suggest them. Each student group will prepare a two- to five-minute conversation among their characters, discussing their topic.

Note: *This activity requires fairly advanced thinking skills and might be most appropriate for older students or selected groups of students in each grade, rather than for all students in a given class.*

★ **Depression Collages.** Provide poster board, old magazines, scissors, glue, crayons and markers and access to computer clip-art software if possible. Have students create collages of words and images that represent the Great Depression. Display collages in the classroom and discuss the images.

★ Practical Crafts

Note: *Recipes in this section are adapted from Great Depression Recipes Web site, www.geocities.com/ NapaValley/1918/great.html.*

★ **Meat(less) Loaf.** Arrange for use of a home economics room or school kitchen and try making this substitute for meat loaf, used during the depression. This recipe will make six small servings. You will need:

 1 cup cooked rice
 1 cup crushed peanuts
 1 cup cottage cheese
 1 egg
 1 tablespoon oil
 1 teaspoon salt

- Combine all ingredients. Bake in a loaf pan at 350° for 30 minutes, or until loaf is firm.

★ **Feed Sack Clothing.** In *The Seventeenth Child* and several other bibliography titles, we learn that poor families sometimes made clothing out of used feed sacks. Mabel Walthall's family felt lucky to get colored sacks so the shirts and dresses were not all brown. Divide the class into four teams, and provide each with the equivalent of two feed sacks (about 18" x 144") of coarsely woven linen or cotton fabric along with scissors, pins, needles and thread. Challenge each team to come up with the best shirt or dress they can using

the materials at hand. Then have a team member model the clothing and let the class vote on the best in feed-sack fashion! (If students complain, point out that you could have assigned them to make underwear from the fabric as many depression families did!)

★ **Mashed Potato Cake.** Farm families loved their sweets! During depression days, cooks got creative and found ways to use what they had on hand to make tasty desserts. Head for the kitchen again and try this unusual recipe. The ingredients you will need are:

> 4 eggs
> 1 scant cup of butter
> 2 cups sugar
> 1 cup mashed potatoes
> 2 ½ cups flour
> 2 teaspoons baking powder
> ½ cup cocoa powder
> 1 tablespoon cinnamon
> 1 teaspoon nutmeg
> 1 teaspoon cloves
> ½ cup milk
> 1 teaspoon vanilla
> 1 cup chopped nuts

• Beat eggs, butter and sugar until creamy. Add mashed potatoes and blend well. Sift flour once, add baking powder and sift again. Add cocoa, cinnamon, nutmeg and cloves to flour mixture. Add flour mixture and milk alternately to the first four ingredients. Mix well. Add vanilla and nuts and stir until blended. Pour into greased cake pans and bake at 350° for 35–45 minutes. When a toothpick inserted into the center comes out clean and the top of the cake springs back when pressed lightly with a finger, it's done.

★ Research Projects

Invite students to use these opportunities to explore the period from 1929–1941 as individual or small group projects, or involve the whole class.

★ **Oral History of the Depression.** *The Seventeenth Child* is a good example of oral history. Assign students to interview someone who lived through the depression. An elderly family member would be ideal, but it could be a neighbor, family friend or resident of a senior housing complex or nursing home. The reproducible worksheet on page 72 will guide the interviews. Students may either tape their interviews or write the responses on paper. Invite students to share their experiences with the class.

★ **Environmental Issues.** Environmental awareness in the 1930s was not what it is today, though the same tensions existed between proponents of economic progress and defenders of natural ecosystems. Have interested students read *Fire on the Wind*, the poem "The Path of Our Sorrow" in *Out of the Dust* and references to the dust bowl in *A Multicultural Portrait of the Great Depression* and *Growing up in the Great Depression*. Then have students research and write reports on either the Tillamook Burn or the dust bowl, addressing these ideas:

• What caused these environmental disasters?

• What is the condition of those damaged ecosystems today?

• What do loggers or farmers do differently today, because of lessons learned from these and other disasters?

• Find evidence of similar conflicts between environmentalists and loggers or farmers today, in the form of newspaper or magazine articles debating current farming or logging practices. Bring the articles to class as part of your report.

★ **Who Helped?** Start by reviewing *Leah's Pony.* During hard times like the depression, people found creative ways to help each other. We read about many ways of helping in the books in this chapter. Penny auctions like the one in *Leah's Pony,* "rent parties," communal soup pots in shantytowns, government aid programs and personal intervention as in *A Letter to Mrs. Roosevelt* all demonstrated generosity, compassion and the strength of family and community. Have students research ways that families, neighbors, communities, organizations and government helped people get through the depression. Students will report their findings to the class with examples, from this chapter's books or other resources, of people who benefited from different kinds of help.

Mystery Phrase Game

Solve the puzzle by first filling in the blanks in each sentence. Then unscramble the circled letters to find the mystery phrase relating to the depression.

1. Farmers who didn't own land, but worked for a portion of the crop were called
   __ __ Ⓞ __ __ __ __ __ __ __ __ __ __ __ __ __.

2. __ Ⓞ __ __ __ __ __   __ __ __ __ __ __ __ __ __ __ was one
   of the most admired First Ladies of all times.

3. During the depression, many people placed __ __ __ Ⓞ __ __ __ __ __ __ in
   their shoes to cover up holes in the soles.

4. Makeshift camps set up to house migrant workers were called
   __ __ __ __ __ __ __ __ __ __ __ Ⓞ __, after the President at the
   beginning of the depression.

5. __ __ __ __ __   __ Ⓞ __ __ __ __ tried to organize laborers to join
   together to improve working conditions.

6. The region of the Central Plains most affected by the droughts of the 1930s was called the
   __ __ __ __   __ __ Ⓞ __.

7. In the cities, hungry people waited in __ __ Ⓞ __ __   __ __ __ __ __
   to receive food from local charity organizations.

Unscramble the circled letters to find the mystery term and write it below:

__ __ __ __   __ __ __ __

Oral History Project

Use these questions to guide your interview with someone who lived through the Great Depression. You might interview an elderly family member, neighbor, family friend or resident of a senior citizen housing complex or nursing home. Feel free to ask additional questions of your own. The idea is to talk with, learn from and share with your classmates the experiences of a veteran of this difficult period in our nation's history.

• How old were you when the stock market crashed in 1929? _____

• What, if anything, do you remember about the stock market crash itself? _____
_____

• Where did you live during the depression? (In a city, small town or on a farm?) _____
_____

• Did you work or go to school during that time? _____
_____

• What kind of work did you or your family do to earn money? _____
_____

• Did anyone in your family lose a job or their home during the depression? _____
_____

• Did your family have trouble living and paying the bills because of the depression? _____
_____

• Did your family have to move around the country or split up during the depression? _____
_____

• Did you know anyone who worked for one of the "New Deal" federal programs, like the CCC or the WPA? _____

• What did your family eat during that time? _____
_____

• What did you do for fun and entertainment? _____
_____

• What did you learn from living through the depression? How do you think it affected your life?
_____
_____

World War II

Though World War I had thrust the U.S. onto the world stage, Americans were reluctant players. Struggling with depression woes at home, many narrowed their sights to the country's own problems while the government took an isolationist approach to world affairs. Even the worrisome successes of authoritarian dictators like Mussolini, Hitler and Hirohito failed to move Americans to join the conflicts spreading throughout Europe, Asia and Africa. President Roosevelt wanted Americans to assist in what was shaping up to be the global defense of democracy, but couldn't raise enough support for entering the war. By the time the Japanese bombed Pearl Harbor in 1941 and forced us into the war, the global picture was dire and only England remained as a viable opponent to the horrors of Nazi Germany and the Axis powers.

Still, once engaged, Americans put their hearts into the war effort. American troops poured onto the various fronts; American factories geared up for wartime production; American women went to work to keep the newly thriving economy going; and American children participated in safety drills, victory gardens and salvage drives. Americans bought war bonds, put up blackout curtains and used ration coupons. The entertainment industry produced radio programs, newsreels, movies, songs and live entertainment to maintain patriotic fervor. The war affected every aspect of American life, unifying and invigorating a disheartened people. Soldiers who died or were wounded in battle were glorified as heroes.

Finally, the highly controversial American decision to end the war with the fearsome atomic bomb, and the beginnings of the Cold War, which resulted from end-of-war tensions, gave Americans and the world much to ponder about our collective future.

Some themes of this period to explore through literature include:

★ America as "the arsenal of democracy:" Economic boon and industrial miracle.

★ Major battles and events of the war.

★ Products and propaganda in the first "media war."

★ War support efforts on the home front.

★ Unprecedented opportunities for women at home.

★ Persistent segregation and discrimination in the military and at home.

★ Executive Order 9066: Internment of Japanese Americans.

★ Use of the atomic bomb and the aftermath of war.

These series might supplement your exploration:

★ The American Scene. Grolier Educational Corporation. 6–8.

★ First Books. Franklin Watts. *Note: Several titles on World War II.* 6–8.

★ The G. I. Series. Chelsea House Publishers. 5–8.

★ World War II. Thomson Learning. 5–8.

Fiction

★ **The Art of Keeping Cool** by Janet Taylor Lisle. Atheneum Books for Young Readers, 2000. 5–8. ALSC Notable Children's Book. While his father flies bombers in Europe, Robert and his mother and sister join his father's family in Rhode Island. Robert's life there provides unexpected challenges—his bullying, authoritarian grandfather; his talented but eccentric cousin; the mystery of his father's estrangement from the family; and the unfolding drama of a German artist accused of spying for the Nazis. A sobering look at the dangers of prejudice, suspicion and mob mentality, as well as family secrets. Highly relevant today.

★ **Baseball Saved Us** by Ken Mochizuki. Lee & Low Books, 1995. 4–6. "Shorty," a Japanese American boy, tells of his family's forced move to an internment camp during World War II. When the stresses of camp life threaten to damage character and relationships, Shorty's father creates a diversion in the form of a baseball field. Baseball not only "saves" the people in the camp, but also helps Shorty find confidence and acceptance upon returning to his home and school after the war. This title presents younger students with similar issues to those in *Under the Blood-Red Sun*.

★ **The Cookcamp** by Gary Paulsen. Bantam Doubleday Dell, 1992. 5–8. With his father away at war and his mother working in a Chicago factory, the boy is sent to his grandmother who cooks for a road crew in northern Minnesota. Only five years old, he doesn't understand everything around him. But he understands the love and affection of his grandmother and the road crew. Life would be grand, if only he didn't miss his mother so. This touching, happy-sad story offers an unusual look at the impact of the war and some of its less-discussed casualties—marital fidelity, family unity and childhood security.

★ **Easter Parade** by Eloise Greenfield. Hyperion Books for Children, 1998. 4–5. Two young cousins in different American cities approach Easter of 1943 with very different feelings. Leanna knows only the anticipation of pretty new clothes and a parade; Elizabeth fears for her soldier father, whose letters have stopped coming. Intimate details of the two girls' lives bring into focus the daily lives of American children during the war. A warm, evocative little book for young readers.

★ **Friends and Enemies** by LouAnn Gaeddert. Atheneum Books for Young Readers, 2000. 5–8. William, a preacher's kid, settles with his family at their new assignment in a small Kansas town just in time to begin high school. He quickly makes friends with Jim, a Mennonite boy in his class. When the Japanese bomb Pearl Harbor and patriotic fever overtakes the community, Jim and his pacifist family come under attack as cowards. William is caught in the middle. A powerful story with much to ponder about friendship, freedom and the courage of convictions.

★ **The Gadget** by Paul Zindel. HaperCollins, 2001. 6–8. Traumatized by the Nazi bombing of London, 13-year-old Stephen is sent to his father in America. Dr. Orr is a physicist working at Los Alamos on a top-secret project intended to bring an end to the war. Stephen, motivated by runaway curiosity and goaded by his friend Alexei, asks forbidden questions and defies the rules to discover the nature of "the gadget." A suspenseful, action-packed look at the development of the atom bomb, including the nightmare awareness of having opened Pandora's box. Great historical detail, with endnotes about the Manhattan Project.

★ **Good Night, Maman** by Norma Fox Mazer. HarperCollins, 2001. 6–8. A little-known episode of World War II involved a shipload of European refugees, mostly Jewish, brought to America at FDR's request. In this book Karin and Marc Levi flee Paris with their mother and go into hiding after their father is arrested. The mother, too sick to travel, sends them on to relative safety. Their trip to America on the refugee ship and their months in the refugee camp in Oswego, New York, are recorded in intimate detail in Karin's letters to her mother. A sad, sweet, growing-up story featuring convincing and appealing characters.

★ **The Morning Glory War** by Judy Glassman. Dell, 1993. 4–6. During fifth grade Jeannie Newman is moved into the "smart class," separating her from her friends and putting her in competition with the teacher's pet. Their rivalry is focused on a newspaper drive to support the war effort. In the meantime, Jeannie's serviceman pen pal, arranged through school, gets the idea she's in high school and writes her a love letter, creating a dilemma. A lightweight look at "normal" life during the war to balance heavier titles on the list.

★ *Stepping on the Cracks* by Mary Downing Hahn. William Morrow & Co., 1992. 5–8. Scott O'Dell Historical Fiction Award Book. For sixth graders living a pleasant, simple life in their small town, the war provides complications never imagined. One day Margaret and her friend Elizabeth have few problems bigger than the inevitable class bully; the next they confront agonizingly conflicted feelings as they help a seriously ill deserter from the army while their own brothers fight in Europe. Things become even more confusing as the girls learn about the abusive family lives that produced both the bully and the deserter. Margaret discovers a sobering adult truth— that there is sometimes "no answer, no firm ground to stand on." A troubling, thought-provoking story.

★ *The Summer of My German Soldier* by Bette Greene. Penguin Putnam Books for Young Readers, 1999. 7–8. Twelve-year-old Patty Bergen, a Jew in a predominately Christian small southern town and the victim of an abusive father and a cold, critical mother, is used to being different and feeling inferior. When she befriends and aids a young escaped German prisoner of war she begins to see herself through his eyes, as a person of value. This deeply moving story of friendship, strength and abiding love found in unlikely places can't fail to touch any reader who has ever felt like an outcast. A superb, engrossing story for more mature readers.

★ *The Unbreakable Code* by Sara Hoagland Hunter. Northland, 1996. 4–6. John is afraid to leave his home on the Navajo Reservation. His grandfather helps him find courage and confidence by sharing his experiences as one of the Navajo Code Talkers of World War II. He helped defeat the Japanese and win the war by passing messages in a code based on the Navajo language. An important and little-known story, well told and illustrated.

★ *Under the Blood-Red Sun* by Graham Salisbury. Bantam Doubleday Dell Books for Young Readers, 1995. 6–8. Scott O'Dell Historical Fiction Award Book. Tomi and his Japanese American family have a pleasant life on Oahu. But when the Japanese bomb Pearl Harbor, Tomi's world turns upside down. His family becomes suspect, along with all Japanese Americans. His father and grandfather are arrested and imprisoned. His mother loses her job, bigoted neighbors threaten Tomi and his little sister is terrified. But his family stands strong and his buddies help him endure. A heartbreaking, candid, uplifting story of personal courage and honor in the face of shameful cruelty and injustice.

★ *"Who Was That Masked Man Anyway?"* by Avi. Scholastic, 1992. 4–8. Frankie (a.k.a. Chet Barker, Master Spy) is obsessed by radio superheroes like the Green Hornet and the Lone Ranger, who regularly save the world from evil; so consumed, in fact, that he neglects his schoolwork and lets his imagination take over. His plot to expose the family's boarder as the evil Nazi scientist he must be, and in the process recover his room and marry his teacher off to his wounded brother, brings hilarious and unexpected results. A funny story, told all in dialogue, with much wartime detail and a quirky, engaging protagonist.

Nonfiction

★ *Atom Bomb* by Tom Sedden. Scientific American Books for Young Readers, 1995. 4–8. Students interested in science might enjoy this picture book format introduction to the science behind the atomic bombs that devastated Japan and brought an end to the war. Readers meet the major players, scientific and otherwise, in the development of the bomb and learn about their feelings and the controversies surrounding the project. Brief discussions of spy activity related to the Manhattan Project and of the Children's Memorial in Peace Park at Hiroshima round out the book.

★ *Children of the World War II Home Front* by Sylvia Whitman. Carolrhoda Books, 2001. 4–5. As part of the Picture the American Past series, this title offers younger students a good, accessible overview of life for American kids during World War II. Ample photos and the picture book format invite readers to take in lots of information quickly and easily. Activity ideas and a bibliography increase the book's value to teachers.

★ ***Rosie the Riveter: Women Working on the Home Front in World War II*** by Penny Colman. Crown Publishers, 1998. 5–8. Colman draws the reader in from page one with fascinating, engaging text that features quotes from women who worked during World War II. Photos, posters, political cartoons and supporting end matter that explore the unprecedented opportunities for women workers, their achievements and the widely varied attitudes toward them, enhance the book's research value.

★ ***Sadako and the Thousand Paper Cranes*** by Eleanor Coerr. Putnam, 1999. 4–8. This simple but moving story tells of Sadako Sasaki, a young Japanese girl who died of leukemia as a result of fallout from the atomic bombs dropped on Japan in 1945. While most of the books in this chapter deal directly with life in America during the war, it's important to consider the consequences of America's use of the bombs and to honor the memory of those who died as a result.

★ ***Tell Them We Remember: The Story of the Holocaust*** by Susan D. Bachrach. Econo-Clad, 1999. 5–8. Bachrach uses powerful photos and biographical clips from the lives of children who were victims of the Nazis to personalize this horrifying story that we don't dare forget. The book is an outreach effort of the U.S. Holocaust Memorial Museum in Washington, D.C.

★ ***A Time to Fight Back: True Stories of Wartime Resistance*** by Jayne Pettit. Houghton Mifflin, 1996. 4–8. While illustrations would make this title more appealing, it has a place for its unique presentation of eight real-life young people from different countries, each of whom experienced the war in a unique way. Through words or actions, each expressed his or her opposition to its injustices and horrors. Of particular interest is the story of a young German girl whose father serves in Hitler's army and who tells of terror, loss, hunger and hardship as a victim of Allied aggression.

★ ***Welcome to Molly's World, 1944: Growing up in World War Two America*** by Catherine Gourley. Pleasant Company Publications, 1999. 4–6. This American Girls Collection title is a fascinating scrapbook of everyday city life in the U.S. during the war and aspects of the lives of soldiers, nurses, flyers and others in the thick of the fighting. Visually appealing and highly accessible.

★ ***World War II*** by Tom McGowen. Scholastic, 1996. 4–6. In concise and no-nonsense style, McGowen summarizes the main events of the war on its various fronts. While he does not dwell on issues and root causes, he reflectively traces the origins of the war back to resentment of World War I surrender conditions and makes the transition from the end of World War II to the Cold War. Good basic factual information, nicely punctuated with photos and maps.

Other Media

★ ***The Devil's Arithmetic*** screenplay by Robert J. Avrech. Showtime Entertainment, 1999 (videocassette). 7–8. This powerful, harsh depiction of the suffering of Polish Jews in a Nazi death camp is not for the very young or the squeamish, though one could argue that many children see a parallel level of "entertainment violence" regularly on television. Based on Jane Yolen's award-winning book, it focuses on Hannah, a contemporary American teen who is bored by her family's old stories and religious traditions. At a Passover Seder, Hannah is mysteriously transported to a Polish shtetl in the 1940s, where she connects with ancestors from the time and experiences the horrors of the Holocaust with them. The video version is graphic and brutal at times, showing, for example, a hanging and the unthinkable reality of the gas chambers. But the violence is hardly gratuitous and will touch more mature students. You might want to inform parents of your plans to show the video. The book, lacking the dramatic visual impact, is more circumspect and gentle, and therefore appropriate for younger students.

★ ***Lily's Crossing*** by Patricia Reilly Giff, narrated by Christina Moore. Recorded Books, 1997 (audiocassettes). 4–6. Newbery Honor Book, ALSC Notable Children's Book. Lily loves summers at the ocean, but hates the idea of this summer with only Gram. Her best friend is moving away and her father is going to war. A not always lovable child, Lily's only prospect for a friend is Albert, a Hungarian refugee who has lost his parents and been separated from his sister by war. Their blossoming friendship stretches both of them to face challenges and grow. A startlingly believable and moving story about friendship, family and the danger of lies.

★ ***Swing out to Victory! Songs of WWII***.
Platinum Entertainment, 1999 (CD). 4–8.
Popular World War II songs make up this fun,
wistful snapshot of life during the war for soldiers and on the home front. They address
issues of rationing, women doing war work
and battle themes. The songs range from
rousing marches to soulful ballads for absent
sweethearts. Such famous names as Bing
Crosby, Glenn Miller and His Orchestra and
Arthur Fiedler and The Boston Pops perform
the songs.

Web sites

★ ***EyeWitness to World War Two***
www.ibiscom.com/w2frm.htm

★ ***GI—World War II Commemoration***
gi.grolier.com/wwii/wwii_mainpage.html

★ ***Lest We Forget: World War II***
geocities.com/Pentagon/9764

★ ***ThinkQuest World War II Homefront
Simulation***
library.thinkquest.org/15511/families/
index.htm

★ ***ThinkQuest Junior World War II: An
American Scrapbook***
tqjunior.thinkquest.org/4616

Activities on World War II

Discussion Prompts

Use these prompts to stimulate discussion of themes and issues of the period.

★ **The War After "The War to End All Wars."** *World War II* and other nonfiction titles in the bibliography review the causes of World War II. Referring to these and other sources, lead a discussion of how the conclusion of World War I led to the outbreak of World War II. The following prompts may be helpful:

- What surrender terms did the Central Powers find excessive and unfair?

- What feelings and attitudes arose in reaction to harsh surrender terms imposed on the Central Powers?

- How did power-hungry leaders take advantage of those feelings and attitudes to further their ambitions? What unlikely alliances did these leaders form to advance their causes?

- What other factors contributed to the conflicts that developed into World War II?

- How did the victorious Allies behave differently at the end of World War II, showing that they had learned from the mistakes of World War I?

★ **Topic for Debate.** Both *Stepping on the Cracks* and *Friends and Enemies* address the issue of pacifists in wartime. Have students read one or both of these titles. Then divide the class in half, assigning one group the affirmative and one the negative side of this question: Would you support the refusal of a pacifist, acting on his or her beliefs, to fight in time of war? Have each side prepare their best arguments, based on the information in these books. Then moderate a lively debate of this important question. Be sure the discussion addresses the issues of courage vs. cowardice, freedom of belief and protecting the rights of all.

★ **An Afternoon with My Favorite Character.** Have each student read at least one selection from the bibliography. Students will choose a real or fictional character from the reading with whom they'd like to spend an afternoon. Use the reproducible worksheet on page 81 to help students prepare for the discussion by clarifying

their reasons for choosing that character, considering how they would spend time with that character and developing questions they would ask the character. Let each student briefly present the information on his or her worksheet and discuss what students have learned about World War II from these characters.

Games

★ **Crossword Puzzle.** Enjoy the crossword puzzle found on the reproducible handout on page 82, based on terms and phrases used during this period. You might consider providing a word bank for younger students.

★ **Baseball.** As we learn in *Baseball Saved Us*, *Under the Blood-Red Sun* and *Welcome to Molly's World, 1944*, baseball was important during the war as a distraction and a way to feel normal in very abnormal circumstances. Enlist the help of a Physical Education teacher or softball or baseball coach to get up a game. Encourage students to think about what playing ball meant to Tomi, Shorty or other World War II–era Americans.

Artistic/Creative Expressions

★ **Create a Radio Superhero.** Review *"Who Was That Masked Man Anyway?"* Then form production teams of two to four students. Each team will create its own World War II era radio superhero and write a radio script, telling an exciting adventure appropriate to the time. Scripts should take three to five minutes to read. Teams will assign roles, rehearse their scripts and take turns reading their scripts for the class.

★ **Design a Poster.** Have students create World War II era posters, like those pictured in *Rosie the Riveter* or mentioned in *Lily's Crossing* and *Friends and Enemies*. Posters might recruit military nurses or women workers for the war effort, warn citizens about careless talk informing enemy spies or urge them to buy war bonds or participate in salvage drives. Have students share and explain their posters.

★ **Ceremony of Honor.** Have students develop and present a ceremony using appropriate words (original writings, excerpts from the books, etc.), visuals and music, honoring the memory of victims of the Nazis. Alternatively or in addition, a group of students might develop and present a ceremony honoring soldiers who fought in World War II. You might combine this activity with the local involvement in the war research project described at the bottom of this page.

★ **Journal Entries.** Have students choose one of several possible scenarios related to World War II. Students will imagine themselves in the scenario and write a journal entry reflecting their feelings and experiences. Possible scenarios might include:

- A Japanese American child after hearing about the bombing of Pearl Harbor.

- A young Jew upon being rescued by Allied soldiers from a concentration camp.

- An American woman at the end of the war who has just lost her job to make room for a returning soldier in the workplace.

Practical Crafts

★ **Victory Garden.** During the height of American involvement in the war, about ⅓ of all vegetables grown in the U.S. came from victory gardens that families planted in order to free up food for soldiers overseas. Get students involved planting vegetables in a victory garden, either outside or in pots in the classroom. If there's time to harvest a crop, consider giving the produce to a shelter or food pantry nearby.

★ **World War II Lunch.** Jell-O was new on the scene and a favorite with wartime working moms looking for easy, cheap and interesting foods. Borrow a kitchen to make the Jell-O salad below. Serve it with sliced Spam, play a little World War II music and get a taste of the 1940s! One recipe serves 8. The ingredients you will need are:

    1 package lime Jell-O
    2 cups boiling water
    ½ cup chopped walnuts
    2 tablespoons honey
    2 tablespoons mayonnaise
    8 canned pear halves
    Lettuce

- Mix Jell-O according to package directions. Pour half of the mixture into a quart-size ring mold and chill until set. Mix together nuts, honey and mayonnaise. Spoon mixture into the centers of canned pear halves. Set pear halves on top of chilled Jell-O and pour the remaining gelatin over the top. Chill until set. Unmold the chilled salad and serve on lettuce leaves.

★ **Japanese Karesansui Garden.** To bring some peace and beauty to their stark lives in internment camps, some Japanese Americans created karesansui gardens. These dry landscape gardens came from Zen Buddhist tradition, using sand to represent flowing water and stones to represent hills or islands. Have students create their own unique karesansui gardens. You may want to provide the sand, the forks or combs and a variety of small stones, or invite students to bring in stones with interesting shapes or colors. Have students:

- Find and bring a small, shallow container to class. Cardboard or plastic trays or boxes work well.

- Fill the container about ¾ full of sand.

- Use a fork or wide-tooth comb to rake the sand into wavy patterns that represent flowing water.

- Bring or choose two to four stones with interesting shapes and arrange them in the sand to look like hills beside the water or islands in the water.

- Rake the sand in circles around the stones to resemble land around the hills or ripples around the islands. The final arrangement should be pleasing to the eye.

- As a restful activity, you can occasionally change the arrangement of your karesansui garden or rake the sand to create new wave patterns.

Research Projects

Invite students to use these opportunities to explore the World War II period as individual or small group projects, or involve the whole class.

★ **Local Involvement in the War.** Have students identify any World War II memorials or museums in the area, or visit the public library or local newspaper for records of community

involvement in the war. A class trip to a local World War II site might result. Invite a war veteran to visit the classroom. Your guest might share his or her war experiences and show uniforms, medals, newspaper clippings or other memorabilia of the war. You might combine this activity with the Ceremony of Honor on page 78, holding the ceremony while your guest is present.

★ **Map Activity.** Invite students to research the geography of the war, using and developing maps that track the action. One student or group might concentrate on major war action before American involvement, while another student or group focuses on the action after 1941; or you could assign students or groups of students to focus on the European front, Africa or Asia with the Pacific. Students should be able to point out Allied and Axis countries, borders that shifted during the war as areas were occupied and liberated and the location of major battle action. A good place to start is the *World War II* title from the bibliography.

★ **Home Front Salvage Drives.** Several of the books, including *The Morning Glory War, Children of the World War II Home Front* and *Stepping on the Cracks,* mention Americans saving, salvaging and turning in everyday items to be recycled into weapons, ammunition or other products in support of the war. Have students study what items were collected and how they were used (e.g., nylon and silk stockings to make parachutes or tow

ropes—see *Rosie the Riveter,* chapter two). Students should report to the class, using charts or other visual aids to illustrate their presentations.

★ **World War II Weapons.** Invite students interested in science to read *Atom Bomb* and/or *The Gadget.* Have them study the workings of these first nuclear weapons and explain the basic scientific principles to the class.

★ **Wartime Entertainment.** Americans at home and abroad needed fun and recreation to help them escape the stresses of the war. Have students research wartime entertainment by looking into one or more of the following subjects:

- World War II Hollywood: Movies and celebrities of the 1940s.

- Radio shows for family entertainment.

- USO productions at home and overseas.

- The All-American Girls Professional Baseball League.

- Popular Music: Songs and dances of the 1940s.

Students should report back with visuals, recordings or live performances, if possible, as examples of the kinds of entertainment available during World War II. A good starting point is *Welcome to Molly's World, 1944.*

An Afternoon with My Favorite Character

Read at least one selection from the bibliography. Then choose a real or fictional character from your reading with whom you would most like to spend an afternoon. Use this worksheet to prepare for class discussion of your ideas for spending an afternoon with this character.

The character I chose: _____

The book in which I found my character: _____

Why I chose this character: _____

_____

_____

How I would spend an afternoon with this character: _____

_____

_____

What questions would I ask this character? _____

_____

_____

_____

What I've learned about World War II from reading about this character: _____

_____

_____

_____

World War II Crossword Puzzle

Complete the crossword puzzle below, using terms from America's involvement in World War II.

Across

3. Victims of Nazi Germany along with Jews, communists, Polish Catholics and others

5. Wartime posters warned that "Loose lips ___ ships."

6. British Prime Minister during World War II

7. Movie houses showed these to update citizens and promote support for the war

8. Italian dictator who joined forces with Hitler and Hirohito to form the Axis

9. "Rosie the ____," symbol of American women working in war factories

10. American families grew vegetables in ___ gardens.

11. American president who ordered use of the atomic bomb on Japanese cities

Down

1. The U.S. earned the title "___ of democracy" for our contribution of weapons and ammunition to the Allies.

2. Japanese Americans were locked up in ___ camps after the bombing of Pearl Harbor.

4. The official name of Hitler's political party, the National _____ German Worker's Party, was shortened to "Nazi."

9. _____ coupons were issued to regulate the amount of certain goods Americans could buy during the war.

The Fifties and Sixties ★

This period simmered with political and social tensions that often erupted in violence at home or abroad. The post–World War II economy boomed and created a state of unprecedented affluence and consumerism. Middle- and upper-class Americans eagerly enjoyed the benefits of new technology. But many poor families and minorities struggled to recover from wartime losses. While Americans understood the policy of containment that involved us in the Korean War, we were tired of war and the unwinnable conflict lost support. Meanwhile at home, schoolchildren were practicing "duck and cover" and convincing their parents to build bomb shelters in fear of attack by evil Communist Soviets. The space race began as another expression of U.S.–Soviet competition. And the largely peaceful protests of the early Civil Rights movement were stirring up the nation too quickly for some and too slowly for others.

Tensions escalated in the 1960s. The nation was captivated by charismatic President Kennedy and his picture book family, then devastated by his assassination. The U.S. became more deeply embroiled in the long and highly controversial Vietnam Conflict, which seemed to many just another unwinnable civil war far from home and which sparked a grassroots antiwar movement unlike anything this nation had seen. The Civil Rights movement became increasingly violent with the assassination of Malcolm X, the emergence of the Black Panther party and the assassination of Martin Luther King, Jr. creating race riots in the streets. Women activists, participating in Civil Rights and anti-war activities, began to champion the rights of women through the Feminist Movement. Through it all the expanding media presented Americans with contrasting pictures—promoting a romanticized image of wholesome, traditional middle-class white family life on one hand, while bombarding the public with graphic images of war, violence, hippies and the emerging drug culture on the other.

Exciting and vital, dangerous and deeply troubled, this period of tragic drama and idealistic hope found a symbolic apex in the 1969 moon walk of astronauts Armstrong and Aldrin.

Some themes and issues of this period to explore through literature include:

★ The Cold War.

★ The Korean War.

★ Racism and the Civil Rights movement.

★ Rock and roll and the development of pop culture.

★ Important figures and leaders of the time.

★ The role of the media.

★ Space exploration.

★ Vietnam and the antiwar movement.

★ The beginnings of the women's liberation movement.

★ Flower power: Disaffected youth and the hippie movement.

These series might supplement your exploration of the period:

★ The American Scene. Grolier Educational Corporation. 6–8.

★ First Books. Franklin Watts. **Note:** *Titles on the Korean War and the Vietnam War.* 6–8.

★ History of Rock and Roll by Stuart A. Kallen. Lucent Books. 4–6.

★ The Young Oxford History of Women in the United States, Volumes 9 and 10. Oxford University Press. 7–8.

Resources on the Fifties and Sixties

Fiction

★ *And One for All* by Theresa Nelson. Orchard Books, 1989. 5–8. Twelve-year-old Geraldine's world is defined by her loving family and her brother's best friend Sam, whom she has always loved. But in 1967 her world begins to unravel. Her brother Wing quits school to join the marines and goes to Vietnam. Back home, Sam becomes an active antiwar protester, alienating himself from Geraldine's family. When Wing dies in combat, Geraldine is forced to confront her conflicted feelings and loyalties. A thought-provoking story full of sympathetic characters.

★ *The Baby Grand, the Moon in July, and Me* by Joyce Annette Barnes. Dial Books for Young Readers, 1994. 4–5. Neil Armstrong is about to walk on the moon and Annie dreams of being an astronaut just like him. But during the historic days of the *Apollo 11* mission, Annie has a mission of her own—to reconcile her family which is split over her brother's dream to be a jazz pianist. Likable Annie's gumption should win the hearts of readers.

★ *Belle Teal* by Ann M. Martin. Scholastic, 2001. 4–7. Belle can't wait for fifth grade when she will be in Miss Casey's class. But the year brings unexpected challenges when the school is in an uproar over forced integration. Belle's friendship with Darryl, an African American boy new to the class, creates a bewildering rift with former friends, and the racial tension turns ugly. Darryl's quiet strength, Belle's fierce loyalty and conviction about what's right and the strong support of her teacher and family lend hope and victory to this sometimes sad, troubling story.

★ *Freedom School, Yes!* by Amy Littlesugar. Philomel Books, 2001. 4–8. In 1964, 600 young volunteers participated in the Mississippi Summer Project, teaching African Americans literacy skills and black history, and helping them register to vote. In this novel, Jolie's family agrees to house Annie, the white Freedom School teacher, and finds their home and church under attack by racists as a result. The courage and determination of Annie and the community to carry on and rebuild help Jolie find strength and pride in herself. An inspiring, well-illustrated picture book.

★ *Heroes* by Ken Mochizuki. Lee & Low Books, 1995. 4–8. Japanese American Donnie is hurt and confused when his friends insist on playing war, with him as the enemy because he "looks like them." His father, a World War II veteran, and his uncle who was decorated for service in Korea, dismiss his indirect appeals for help out of humility and disenchantment with war. But when the problem escalates, Donnie's family finds a way to show his friends that heroes come in many "colors." An impactful and timely message.

★ *Long Time Passing* by Linda Crew. Delacorte Press, 1997. 7–8. This would be an ordinary adolescent romance except for two things. First, the rich 1960s setting of political upheaval and social change and their impact on high school life rings true. Second, the main characters are well drawn, believable and likable without being too perfect. Ultimately, it's the story of Kathy's evolution into a strong, independent young woman able to stand up for herself and make good decisions, even in the heady context of first love. Recommended for more mature readers, as issues of drugs and sex are dealt with in frank, though sensitive and responsible, ways.

★ *Music from a Place Called Half Moon* by Jerrie Oughton. Bantam Doubleday Dell Books for Young Readers, 1995. 6–8. Edie Jo is a normal 13-year-old—sometimes brooding, sometimes childlike—and beginning to wonder who she is and what she thinks. When smoldering prejudice between whites and Native Americans flares up and her father takes a stand for integration, Edie Jo ponders her position. She stumbles into a friendship with a Native American boy and with the friendship comes troubling knowledge about deadly fires set in town. Edie Jo's ability to know and trust her heart and to take a stand against prejudice endears her to readers and transforms tragedy into hope.

★ *The Outsiders* by S. E. Hinton. Dell, 1967. 7–8. This harsh contemporary classic, written when Hinton was 16, transformed young adult literature by depicting with uncompromising realism the physical and emotional lives of teenage "greasers" and "socs" of the 1960s. Lawlessness and pointless violence, loyalty and posturing among peers, yearning

for love and parental authority and challenges of having too little or too much of what you need are all examined through the tough-but-sensitive eyes of 14-year-old Ponyboy Curtis. An easy read, but a powerful, important book for young people struggling to be what they want to be in spite of labels and prejudices.

★ ***Rosie's Tiger*** by Anna Myers. Walker, 1994. 4–7. Rosie is thrilled that her big brother is coming home safe from the Korean War until she learns that he will bring a Korean wife and son with him. Since their mother died, Ronny has been the most important person in the world to Rosie and she can't bear the thought of sharing him. Only a crisis that endangers little Yon So alters her determination to drive Ronny's Korean family away. Through it all, Rosie learns about prejudice, friendship, magic, truthfulness and accepting life and people as they come.

★ ***Smoky Night*** by Eve Bunting. Harcourt Brace, 1994. Caldecott Medal Book. 4–8. Bunting tells of a night of race rioting, looting and arson in an inner city neighborhood. Neighbors of different ethnic backgrounds have avoided each other before, preferring "their own people." But the tragic events bring people together and open the door to trust and friendship. Glorious, vibrant paintings and collages by David Diaz capture the drama, violence and hope of the story. A powerful, emotional experience for all ages.

★ ***When Zachary Beaver Came to Town*** by Kimberly Willis Holt. Bantam Doubleday Dell, 2001. 5–8. ALSC Notable Children's Book. Holt tells of a memorable summer in Antler, Texas, where predictable routines are disrupted by the arrival of Zachary Beaver, "Fattest boy in the World." Thirteen-year-old Toby and his buddy Cal start out gawking at the "freak." But through the summer, in a deft parade of quirky characters and inter-weaving plot lines, friendships develop and change in unexpected ways and the boys learn about getting past the surface and accepting what life offers. Full of Vietnam era detail.

Nonfiction

★ ***The 1950s: From the Korean War to Elvis*** by Stephen Feinstein. Enslow Publishers, 2000. 4–8. Written in breezy prose and packed with black-and-white photos, this Decades of the 20th Century title is surprisingly substantial. Tackling, in brief but informative essays, everything from *I Love Lucy* to the Korean War, it offers a wonderful overview and starting point for research. *The 1960s: From the Vietnam War to Flower Power,* also by Feinstein, is equally good.

★ ***The 50s*** by Dan Epstein. Chelsea House, 2000. 4–8. The 20th Century Pop Culture series offers a flashy "tabloid" look at American popular culture. Each decade volume (*The 60s* is also written by Epstein) moves year by year, skimming the surface of popular trends in movies, music, cars, fashion, food fads, TV, literature, art, recreation, toys and inventions. Slick and fun.

★ ***Great African Americans in Civil Rights*** by Pat Rediger. Crabtree Publishing, 1996. 4–7. This Outstanding African Americans series title introduces 13 African American leaders in the fight for Civil Rights. While the brief profiles are unavoidably superficial—especially a problem with a figure as controversial and complex as Malcolm X—they aim for a fair, balanced tone. Full of photos, quotes and summary charts, the book is a good starting point for research.

★ ***Joseph McCarthy and the Cold War*** by Victoria Sherrow. Blackbirch Press, 1998. 5–8. This Notorious Americans and Their Times series title strives for an objective tone but finds little good to say about the Wisconsin senator responsible for the 1950s witch-hunt for communists in American life and government. Readers may wonder how such a deceptive, manipulating, blundering character could spark such frenzy and build such a following. But the Cold War context is deftly sketched and the cautionary message well delivered. This may be of particular interest to students who enjoy studying "the bad guys."

★ ***A Multicultural Portrait of the Vietnam War*** by David K. Wright. Benchmark Books, 1996. 5–8. Like other books in the Perspectives series, this title focuses on the participation of women and minorities in its target era. While carefully examining the background of the war and the issues at stake, it concentrates on the human implications. It explores who fought and died; how they were treated in battle and at home; who opposed the war; and the impact of media coverage, corruption and scandal in Vietnam and the U.S. on soldiers and the outcome of American involvement. A worthy research tool.

★ *Oh, Freedom! Kids Talk about the Civil Rights Movement with the People Who Made It Happen* by Casey King and Linda Barrett Osborne. Alfred A. Knopf, 1997. 4–8. In chapters that deal with life under segregation, the movement to end legal segregation and the struggle to end poverty and discrimination, this book approaches public events in personal ways. Students share brief interviews with family or community members who participated in the Civil Rights movement of the '50s and '60s. The militant black nationalist movement is featured along with Martin Luther King, Jr.'s nonviolent campaign, and while most interviewees are African American, "rainbow" participants in the movement are reflected in the stories of whites, Latinos and Japanese Americans as well. While interviews are sometimes superficial, the students' involvement in the process is engaging.

★ *Rachel Carson* by Eve Stwertka. Franklin Watts, 1991. 4–6. During the '50s and '60s the environmental movement was beginning to find its voice. In this well-written biography of pioneering woman scientist, ecologist and writer Rachel Carson, Stwertka tells of her great dedication to and powerful impact on efforts to treat our physical environment with foresight, respect and responsibility.

★ *Shake, Rattle & Roll: The Founders of Rock & Roll* by Holly George-Warren. Houghton Mifflin, 2001. 4–8. George-Warren and illustrator Laura Levine have created an information-packed introduction to 14 of rock and roll's earliest stars. In dynamic two-page spreads they highlight the lives, influence and careers of Bill Haley, Elvis, LaVerne Baker, Buddy Holly and many more. An intelligent, lively and appealing picture book with background on the origins of the music of at least two generations.

★ *The Way Things Never Were: The Truth about the "Good Old Days"* by Norman H. Finkelstein. Atheneum Books for Young Readers, 1999. 5–8. Finkelstein debunks myths about how much better and simpler life was in the 1950s and '60s. Chapters deal with health, diet, environmental concerns, family life, crime, transportation, the elderly and school life. The book uses black-and-white photos, statistics and quotes to make the case that our lives are better today than ever before. An interesting look at the impact of technology and social awareness on the lives of children then and now.

★ *When John & Caroline Lived in the White House* by Laurie Coulter. Hyperion, 2000. 4–8. Lavishly illustrated with photos, this picture book tells of the famous "1,000 days" of the reign of the Kennedy family over America's hearts. The family is pictured as close and affectionate and Jackie Kennedy's effort to protect a sense of normalcy in her children's lives is evident. Everyday family life coexists with events of global impact, and the family's response to the President's death is shared with dignity and touching emotion.

★ Other Media

★ *Casey Kasem Presents America's Top 10 Through the Years: 1950s*. Top Sail Productions, 2001 (CD). 4–8. This CD presents 20 top rock and roll hits of the decade performed by the original artists. The collection features Bill Haley and the Comets, Buddy Holly and the Crickets, Little Richard and Jerry Lee Lewis, among others. A sister recording (similar title) for the 1960s features the Supremes, the Beach Boys, Aretha Franklin, the Mamas and the Papas and more. Fun listening.

★ *Our Friend, Martin: A Magical Movie Adventure Inspired by the Life of Martin Luther King, Jr.* Twentieth Century Fox, 1999 (videocassette). 4–6. This time-travel fantasy combines animation with live footage from the life of Dr. King. Sixth-graders on a field trip visit King's childhood home and are transported back in time, dropping into his life at critical moments of the Civil Rights movement. When they bring King into the future to save him from the assassin's bullet they know is coming, they get an unsettling vision of what our time might have become without the sacrifices of Civil Rights leaders of the 1960s. Stereotyped characters are appropriate to the cartoon format, and the impressive cast of celebrity voices and musical performers makes this a fun way to experience and understand the message of King's dream.

★ *The Wall* by Eve Bunting, hosted by Levar Burton. GPN/WNED-TV, 1992 (videocassette). 4–6. Bunting's book is featured in the first segment of this Reading Rainbow episode. Along with the book's story of a young boy and his father visiting the Vietnam Veteran's Memorial in honor of the grandfa-

ther who died in Vietnam, the episode interviews Maya Lin, the architect who designed the wall, and takes viewers on a visit there. The combination is a powerful tribute to those who served and died, without sanctioning the war itself.

★ ***The Watsons Go to Birmingham: 1963*** by Christopher Paul Curtis, read by LeVar Burton. Bantam Doubleday Dell Audio Publishing, 1995 (audiocassettes). 4–8. Newbery Honor Book. Ten-year-old Kenny's family bubbles over with love, laughter, teasing and the tensions of growing up in troubled times. Concern for Kenny's "juvenile delinquent" brother Byron sends the family to Alabama to visit Grandma, a strict African American woman who, they hope, will straighten Byron out. In Birmingham they experience the horror of a racist bombing of a black church. Kenny's terror for his sister in the church and his shame at fleeing the scene cause him to withdraw in numb bewilderment. It is Byron who helps Kenny cope and move

on, in a heartrending triumph of family love over evil and despair. A masterwork of both writing and reading, wrapping deadly serious content in a hilarious, rowdy, endearing package. An epilogue summarizes the Civil Rights movement and encourages listeners to be American heroes who stand up for justice.

Web sites

★ ***Rock and Roll Hall of Fame and Museum***
www.rockhall.com/home/default.asp

★ ***Apollo 11 30th Anniversary Site***
nssdc.gsfc.nasa.gov/planetary/lunar/
apollo_11_30th.html

★ ***Fast Attacks & Boomers: Submarines in the Cold War***
americanhistory.si.edu/subs/index.html

★ ***Seattle Times: Martin Luther King Jr.***
seattletimes.nwsource.com/mlk

Activities on the Fifties and Sixties

★ Discussion Prompts

Use these prompts to stimulate discussion of themes and issues of the period.

★ **"Looking Like the Enemy."** In *Heroes,* Donnie's friends thoughtlessly cast him as the enemy in their war games because of his appearance. Help students explore this concept of "looking like the enemy" using these prompts:

- Why does Donnie "look like the enemy" to his friends? What is the historical context for that view?

- Do Japanese, Korean and Vietnamese people look alike to non–Asian Americans? To each other?

- How does Donnie feel about being cast as "the enemy?" How do you think being branded generically "Asian," rather than recognized as Japanese American, makes Donnie feel?

- Who might "look like the enemy" to Americans today?

- What do we need to learn from *Heroes* about how we treat people who "look like the enemy?"

★ **Playing War.** In both *Heroes* and *When Zachary Beaver Came to Town,* experienced soldiers express the view that children should not play war games. Review Donnie's father's comments in *Heroes* and Wayne's letter to Cal in chapter 22 of *When Zachary Beaver Came to Town.* Then debate this statement: "It is natural and harmless for children to play war games for fun."

★ **Teenagers.** The term "teenager" came into common use during this period. Before the 1950s, the politics and economics of American life required children and young adults to share the workload, go to work or war at a young age, take on adult responsibilities and grow up in a hurry. The idea of a protected "teen" period between childhood and adulthood didn't exist. By 1950, things were changing and a "teen culture" developed, characterized by independent or rebellious attitudes expressed in clothing, music and leisure activities. Several books in this chapter, including *Long Time Passing,* show this new "teen culture," but *The Outsiders* is important as the first book written by a teen to draw attention to serious problems and pressures of teen life in America. Discuss this new concept of the teen years. *Note: This discussion might work better with older students.*

- Brainstorm ideas about what activities and ideas were common to teens in America in the 1950s and '60s. How about now?

- Find examples in the books that illustrate those ideas and activities.

- What are the most important "jobs" for people during the teen years? What do teens need to learn and accomplish during this time?

- Teens now have more leisure time and more choices than they did in the past. Does that make life easier or harder? Explain your answer.

- What are the best things about being a teenager in America? What are the hardest things?

- *The Outsiders* talks about conflict between "greasers" and "socs." What groups in American schools are at odds today? How are they different from each other, and about what things do they disagree? You might introduce this question by reviewing the first pages of chapter three of *The Outsiders.*

★ Games

★ **Wordsearch Puzzle.** Enjoy the wordsearch puzzle on the reproducible handout on page 92, based on terms used during this period.

★ **Songburst.** Find a copy of the '50s/'60s edition of the game Songburst, and see how well today's students know yesterday's pop music. With the current "retro" popularity of the period, you might be surprised! Just to be sure, consider recruiting a willing music teacher and a few other parents or grandparents from the era to help you out and screen the game cards for likely tunes.

★ **Twister.** This popular game was introduced in 1966. More than 35 years later, it's still fun for all ages and could make a good break for small groups of students in the classroom or during recess or gym. It is widely available in stores and family game closets!

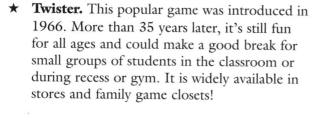

Artistic/Creative Expressions

★ **Protest Posters.** Many young people, including characters in *Long Time Passing* and *And One for All*, participated in antiwar or Civil Rights protests. Based on their reading, have students choose one of the social movements of the 1950s or 1960s and create protest posters with slogans and graphics expressing their feelings about Civil Rights, the antiwar movement, women's liberation or the beginning environmental movement. Students should share and explain their posters. *Oh, Freedom!*, *A Multicultural Portrait of the Vietnam War* and *The 1960s: From the Vietnam War to Flower Power* are good places to start.

★ **Dramatic Reading.** This chapter's books are filled with both drama and humor. Assign each student to find a favorite passage (not to exceed two pages) from one of the books to read to the class as expressively as possible. They should try to make fellow students feel the drama or the humor of the passage. Students may need to "set up" their reading with brief comments about the passages. An example of an excellent dramatic passage is found in chapter 16 of *Music from a Place Called Half Moon*, where Edie Jo's daddy ponders the harm done by prejudice and the need for change. For an example of a humorous passage, read just about any section from the first part of *The Watsons Go to Birmingham: 1963*.

★ **After School at the Malt Shop.** Celebrate the period by planning a party. Invite students to dress like teenagers in the '50s or '60s, play music from the period, find volunteers to demonstrate popular dances of the time and serve appropriate treats. You might use frozen mini White Castle burgers and make malts, shakes and cherry Cokes. Invite students to read aloud profiles of early rock stars from *Shake, Rattle & Roll*, and then play their songs from the *Casey Kasem Presents America's Top 10 Through the Years: 1950s* CDs.

★ **Hippie Love Bus.** Using large paper, create the shape of a van like those of the 1960s to mount on a wall of the classroom or hallway. Have students decorate the bus with hippie symbols and slogans, as though they were preparing to drive it to Woodstock in the summer of 1969. Then discuss the meaning of the symbols and the ideals, both serious and casual, which characterized the hippie movement.

★ **A Family to Follow.** Revisit the activity introduced in chapter one. Have students move forward through the generations and develop a character descended from the original family from chapter one. Then create a story about a day or a week in the character's life. The story might stress ordinary daily activities, describe a holiday or special event in the character's life or show the character involved in some historical event from the '50s or '60s. It might take the form of a short story, poem, song or play. Offer suggestions as needed, but let students take initiative and be creative.

Practical Crafts

★ **Stocking Your Bomb Shelter.** During the Cold War, children encouraged families to prepare bomb shelters in basements or underground cellars. Have students think about their own families and plan what they would include in a bomb shelter survival kit to sustain and entertain them through a bombing attack on their town. Consider food and water, clothing, medical supplies, bedding and things to do to supply the family for a week in a small space. *The 1950s: From the Korean War to Elvis* will get you started.

★ **Homemade Pizza.** Pizza became a favorite in America after World War II. American soldiers returning from Italy brought a taste for Italian flavors. But it wasn't until 1967 that frozen pizza was available at grocery stores. Until then, pizza lovers had to make their own from scratch. Use this simplified recipe to make "homemade" pizza. You'll need to borrow a refrigerator and oven in the school kitchen or home economics room. Divide the class into pairs or small teams, depending on the size of pizza you choose. You'll need:

frozen pizza dough or flour tortillas

canned pizza sauce

a variety of toppings (pepperoni, onions, green peppers, mushrooms, etc.)

grated mozzarella cheese

- Prepare frozen pizza dough according to package directions. If you use tortillas, place them on cookie sheets. Spread canned sauce in an even layer over the dough or tortillas. Add toppings as desired. Cover all with grated cheese. Bake in a 400° oven until dough is cooked, sauce is bubbling and cheese is melted (10–20 minutes). You might serve the pizza with Kool-Aid, Funny Face or Gatorade, all of which were introduced during this period.

Research Projects

Invite students to use these opportunities to explore the period as individual or small group projects, or involve the whole class.

★ **Comparing Korea and Vietnam.** *Heroes* shows children lumping together the Korean War and the Vietnam Conflict in their minds. Have students use this chapter's books and other classroom or media center resources to create a chart comparing and contrasting America's involvement in the Korean War with the Vietnam Conflict. Include columns addressing the dates, location and geography of the two countries, who fought on each side, why we fought, how Americans felt about our involvement, what kinds of tactics and weapons were used, how many Americans served and died, who "won," how our involvement ended and how Americans feel now about each war. Have students summarize their findings in a brief paragraph about how the two wars were similar and different.

★ **Timeline.** Build on the timeline activity introduced in chapter one. Create a timeline cover-

ing major events of the period. Include events related to the Cold War, the Korean War, the Vietnam War, the space race, the Civil Rights movement, the antiwar or feminist movements, the birth of rock and roll, etc. You might assign each student to "nominate" an event for the timeline and to justify their nomination in terms of historical importance.

Review Activity

★ **Exploring U.S. History Issues Over Time.** History doesn't happen in chapters. Just as the Timeline activity and A Family to Follow encouraged students to take a long view and see continuity of issues and concerns as they moved forward through America's history, this activity will help students look back and pull together thoughts about important issues that have persisted throughout our history to date. Use the Issues Over Time reproducible worksheet on page 94 and follow these steps:

- Help each student identify an issue of interest in our country's history that appears in several chapters of this book.

- Help students identify three historical figures from different periods who were actively involved in addressing their issue.

- Assign students to research these figures and their involvement with the issues, using books from the chapter bibliographies or other classroom or media center resources.

- Have students share their findings through oral reports supported by posters or other visual aids. The reports should include brief essays summarizing the progress of the issues through U.S. history and the status of those issues today.

- Example: A student exploring the issue of women's rights might study Abigail Adams, Elizabeth Cady Stanton and Gloria Steinem.

Fifties and Sixties Word Search

Review the bolded words and their definitions on page 93. Then find and circle the words on the grid below. They may read up, down, across, diagonally or backwards.

```
I  N  T  E  G  R  A  T  I  O  N  O  C  B  B
Q  K  Q  E  D  M  P  C  A  O  V  P  W  E  K
U  C  P  R  E  J  U  D  I  C  E  W  V  A  V
C  O  M  M  U  N  I  S  M  Z  T  E  I  T  O
F  T  G  W  S  W  A  K  N  L  E  I  E  N  M
Z  S  K  H  W  J  M  G  F  L  R  P  T  I  U
J  D  M  I  S  S  I  L  E  O  A  P  N  K  M
K  O  N  G  N  T  F  J  M  R  N  I  A  K  Z
B  O  Y  C  O  T  T  V  I  N  S  H  M  X  X
U  W  R  E  K  L  U  N  N  K  A  G  E  V  C
Y  T  S  E  T  O  R  P  I  C  G  C  H  P  J
V  S  K  O  A  Z  B  R  S  O  W  F  O  D  F
N  I  C  B  R  K  T  L  M  R  P  K  A  T  M
I  W  Z  O  A  S  R  G  S  K  Y  N  L  E  V
Y  T  Q  Y  G  W  S  T  I  F  X  Q  R  D  W
```

beatnik

boycott

communism

feminism

hippie

integration

Korea

miniskirt

missile

prejudice

protest

rock 'n roll

sputnik

teenagers

twist

veterans

Vietnam

Woodstock

Fifties and Sixties Word Search Definitions

Beatnik: member of a '50s literary movement that condemned current social morals and stressed individual expression

Boycott: to refuse to support a business or organization in protest

Communism: a political ideology based on communal ownership of property, seen as a great evil that threatened the world in the '50s and '60s

Feminism: social and political movement stressing equality of sexes and promoting women's rights

Hippie: a social movement of youth in the '60s stressing nonviolence and freedom from restrictions

Integration: process of incorporating African Americans into American society as equals

Korea: Asian country where the U.S. and other countries battled Communism in the 1950s

Miniskirt: very short skirt that became popular in the '60s

Missile: a kind of weapon prominent in the '50s and '60s, as in the Cuban Missile Crisis

Prejudice: the practice of judging a person or group without adequate information

Protest: to publicly object to something, e.g., the Vietnam War

Rock 'n roll: a new form of popular music introduced in the '50s

Sputnik: a Russian satellite first launched in 1957 that set off the "Space Race"

Teenagers: term introduced in the '50s to identify youth ages 13 to 20

Twist: a new dance that swept the teen world in the '50s

Veterans: men and women who have served in America's armed forces

Vietnam: Southeast Asian country where the U.S. fought an unpopular war against Communism from 1957–1975

Woodstock: a place in New York famous as the site of a huge rock music festival in 1969

Issues Over Time

This activity will help you follow an important issue that has persisted throughout America's history until now. **For example:** If you explore the issue of women's rights, you might study Abigail Adams, Elizabeth Cady Stanton and Gloria Steinem.

My issue is: _____

Three historical figures involved in my issue are:

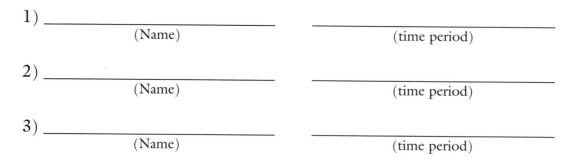

1) _____   _____
            (Name)   (time period)

2) _____   _____
            (Name)   (time period)

3) _____   _____
            (Name)   (time period)

Use this chart to organize your thoughts about the contributions that each person made to your issue. Copy and continue the chart on another sheet if you need more space.

Figure 1	Figure 2	Figure 3

Notes for my essay on the progress of my issue over time and its status today:

_____

_____

_____

_____

_____

Major Award-Winning Titles

An index of the award-winning titles listed in *Pages of the Past*.